THE FINANCIAL MATRIX

AND HOW TO ESCAPE IT

New York Times Bestselling Author

Orrin Woodward

Published by:
Obstaclés Press
200 Commonwealth Court
Cary, NC 27511

orrinwoodward.com

ISBN: 978-0-9983070-1-5

Third Edition, December 2016
10 9 8 7 6 5 4 3

Scripture quotations marked "KJV" are taken from The Holy Bible, Cambridge, 1769.

Scripture quotations marked "NIV" are taken from The Holy Bible, New International Version®, NIV®, Copyright© 1973, 1978, 1984, 2011 by Biblica, Inc.® Used by permission of Biblica, Inc.® All rights reserved worldwide.

Cover and text design by Norm Williams, nwa-inc.com
Printed in the United States of America

Wars in old times were made to get slaves. The modern implement of imposing slavery is debt.

—EZRA POUND

Contents

An investment in knowledge pays the best interest.

—Benjamin Franklin

CHAPTER 1

OUR STORY

Although the life-changing conversation occurred nearly twenty-three years ago, I still remember it as if it were yesterday. I had just walked in the front door from a long day at work when Laurie enthusiastically announced that we were pregnant. Whoa! Talk about an emotional jolt. On one hand, I was pumped, happy to be starting our family. On the other hand, however, I was worried, for my engineering brain quickly calculated the economic implications of Laurie's message, and it didn't look good. Nevertheless, I refused to let my personal worries ruin our festive moment, so I wrapped my arms around Laurie and buried the growing angst as joy and fear battled for emotional supremacy.

Perhaps I need to explain further the mental war raging inside of me. In short, one of my key selling points in convincing Laurie to marry me was my expected income as a successful engineer, an income I believed would allow Laurie to be a stay-at-home mom. Of course, this promise (with many others) was made before we were married and the reality of our financial situation hit us (we had accumulated over thirty-two thousand dollars of consumer debt outside of our mortgage before children). Now, with Laurie's surprise announcement, I had no clue how we were going to make ends meet without her income as an accountant, especially since I knew children could only add more expenses to our already bulging budget. There was simply no way we could lose Laurie's income, add children's expenses, and not fall even further behind financially.

Embarrassingly, however, like the proverbial ostrich with its head in the sand, I refused to face facts. I somehow believed that if I ignored the issue long enough, Laurie would just continue working until we cleaned up our financial mess. In my most optimistic moments, I even convinced myself that Laurie wanted to continue working (after all, she was a professional accountant) and that she wouldn't hold me to promises I had made during the courting process. My optimism, needless to say, was not well-founded. After several weeks of tolerating my strategic silence, Laurie dropped the bomb. Despite her knowing I had to go to class later that night, Laurie flat out asked me when she should tell her employer she was leaving her job to raise our family. This was it. The moment I had hoped to avoid was now upon me, and I could feel my heart rate increasing precipitously.

While not happy with what I perceived was a breach of etiquette, I simply breathed deeply and shared my rehearsed lines about our precarious condition, a financial state that made it impossible for her to leave her job. Laurie, evidently, had rehearsed her lines as well, for she simply said, "Orrin, you promised me." I attempted to explain away this inarguable fact by agreeing with her statement in principle but repeating to her the timing wasn't right. Laurie ignored my rationalizations and merely repeated, "Orrin, you promised me." They say facts are pesky things, and no matter how badly I wanted to dismiss Laurie's facts, the pesky part was she spoke truth. Disoriented,

I suddenly lost my rational posture and meekly mumbled something about unpaid bills and poor timing. Laurie, not buying anything I was selling, stared into my eyes and said one more time, "Orrin, you promised me." That ended the argument—game, set, match to Laurie! How could I argue with her any longer? Humbled, embarrassed, and without any idea of exactly how I was going to do it, I agreed to honor my commitment.

Strangely, I felt relieved after our discussion. Sure, the financial issue wasn't resolved, but the moral one was. I had made a promise, and now I resolved to keep it. Running late for class, I hustled to my car and headed down to my University of Michigan MBA night class. The hour and a half drive was filled with a series of philosophical questions directed at my steering wheel. I asked myself what financial turn I had missed to land in this money mess. No matter how many accolades I had received (honor society in college, four US patents, a National Technical Benchmarking award, to name just a few), I still had to admit I was falling short financially. I realized that if something was going to change, I would need to change something. It was time, in other words, for me to confront the brutal reality of our finances.

Like most other men of my generation, I had learned to diversify my income by sending my wife off to work, but we still lived paycheck to paycheck. I thought, if two upwardly mobile professionals couldn't make ends meet, how was everyone else surviving financially? My rose-colored glasses officially cracked on that drive to class as I wrestled for answers. I vowed to fulfill the promises I had made to Laurie, even if I had to get another job to do so.

Not to sound overly dramatic, but this night was a turning point. I no longer accepted conventional financial wisdom blindly. Instead, I committed to examine the consequences of every financial move and not just do what everyone else was doing. As an engineer, I studied processes and systems by applying cause-and-effect reasoning; ironically, however, while professionally teaching "In God we trust; all others must have data," until that night, I had never thought to apply the same principle in my personal finances. It was time to study the data to determine how to make it financially in the modern world.

Until Debt Do Us Part

Slowly, as I researched the data from people around the world, it dawned upon me that Laurie and I were not the only ones in financial duress. Indeed, most people (between student loans, car loans, credit cards, and home mortgages) are drowning in a sea of debt. Moreover, it's not just personal debt damaging finances of citizens across the globe, for business and government debt is also working against the average household. These three debt drains (personal, business, and government) combine to endanger the financial health of practically every family.

For instance, according to GoBankingRates, an organization that tracks interest and banking rates, in 2014, the average American was more than $225,000 in debt, and almost half of US households had less than $500 in savings. Here is a summary of the American statistics organized by category of debt:

- Average credit card debt among indebted households: $15,263
- Average credit card interest rate: 14.95% APR
- Average mortgage debt: $147,591

- Average outstanding student loan balance: $31,646
- Average auto loan debt: $30,738
- Percentage of Americans with at least $500 in a savings account: 59%*

When the average debt numbers are multiplied by the average interest rates, one arrives at the astounding figure of approximately $1,500 per month (nearly a third of of an average household's income); this is the amount of money that the average family must pay just to service debt. However, servicing debt doesn't decrease debt; it merely pays the interest on the debt. All of this so the household can merely use what it cannot afford to own.

Further, according to Internal Revenue Service (IRS) data, the real (inflation adjusted) median household income for 2013 was $51,939. This may sound impressive until one remembers that total household income has been trending downward (a drop of nearly 8%) since its 1999 peak of $56,895. In other words, the average American has worked the last sixteen years for less income while household debt, product prices, and government taxes have all increased!

Speaking of average incomes, it's important to remember that the average household income is the total incomes of everyone earning in the household. The average person's income is significantly less impressive than the average household's. According to the 2014 IRS data, the average American made just $33,048. Here are the top American percentages:

---

* The data from around the rest of the developed world are equally alarming.

- Top 1% – $380,354
- Top 5% – $159,619
- Top 10% – $113,799
- Top 25% – $67,280
- Top 50% – $33,048

When the average income figures are placed side by side with the average personal debt figures, the modern debt disaster is revealed. Decreasing income and increasing debt is simply not a sustainable plan. Dismally, while the increasing debt load is hurting all ages and incomes within society, the next generation seems to be particularly vulnerable. A recent Wells Fargo study revealed that millennials are spending at least half their monthly paychecks to pay off debt. Furthermore, a University of Arizona study discovered that half of all graduates are still relying on their parents or other family members for financial help two years after graduating.

The Financial Matrix: Choices on Offense and Defense

Perhaps the best way to display how debt is damaging families is to graph each of the possible outcomes a person can experience financially based upon how he/she plays defense (reducing expenses) and offense (increasing income). The Financial Matrix is a 2X2 matrix that displays how the financial results (ownership and choices) a person experiences are directly related to the choices he makes with respect to his income and expenses. True financial freedom, in other words, can only be accomplished by learning to play good financial defense and offense through understanding the rules of the Financial Matrix playing field. Thankfully, anyone can learn the rules of the financial game and change his financial situation just as Laurie and I did.

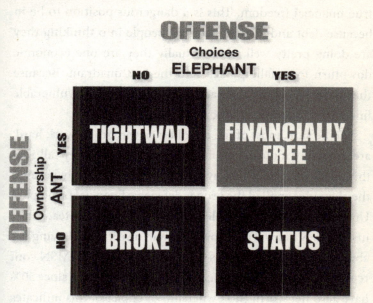

Unbelievably, the latest research reported on economist.com reveals that 50% of Americans (the numbers across the developed world are similar) have *zero* net worth—not even a penny. When debts are subtracted from assets, over 50% of Americans have no ownership, literally nothing to show for years of hard work. This quadrant displays people who do not play financial defense or offense and thus are broke, having no ownership and few choices. Most of these people live, as Henry David Thoreau once wrote, "lives of quiet desperation," believing there is no escape from the Financial Matrix.

The second group in the bottom right quadrant, in contrast, has debt and little ownership, but does enjoy some of the finer things in life. This quadrant does take nice vacations and drive the nicer cars by accumulating debt. The appearance of financial success, evidently, is more important to them than actual success. In short, status through debt substitutes for true financial freedom. This is a dangerous position to be in because debt and choices can fool people into thinking they are doing pretty well when actually they are one economic downturn from falling back into the first quadrant. Because they have debt above their actual incomes, they are vulnerable financially to any economic downturns.

To be sure, most of the members of this group work hard, are upwardly mobile, and are hungry to learn. They fall into this quadrant, the same way Laurie and I did, mainly because they have not applied the proper defensive financial principles. Unfortunately, some people in this group are not teachable; instead they know it all, show it all, and owe it all, believing the ability to accrue debt makes them financial wizards. MSN.com reported that 80% of Americans have debt; therefore, since 50% have zero net worth (no ownership or choices), this indicates that the remaining 30% still have choices (because they have cash flow to borrow more), but have little true ownership. These people do not play good financial defense and instead accumulate debt to pretend they have freedom and lifestyles beyond what they can actually afford. They lease cars, live in highly mortgaged houses, and finance their vacations.

While this plan may appear to work short-term, it's like playing Russian roulette. For if the family suffers a lost job, health, or worst of all, marriage, the debt-based house of cards comes crashing down. Sadly, this is more common than most people realize, because life is unpredictable. For instance, just ask the auctioneers who sell off the goods of once seemingly prosperous families; they know how common it is. Even without an economic downturn, however, compound interest can still catch up to a person's ability to earn and drag him back into the poor house. This is why financial defense is so important because it's the best way to prepare for the inherent risk of living.

This brings us to the top left position, one of the more secure quadrants because these people have learned how to play financial defense. They have ownership, but do not have many choices since they have not learned how to increase their financial offense to live their dreams. Financial offense is more than just a person's income, but also a measure of the potential increase in income over the coming year. After all, if a person's income is flat lined, having little opportunity to increase the following year, then his offensive potential is non-existent. And just like a good football team, both defense and offense are necessary to win.

This quadrant has not learned how to play offense. For example, as an engineer, I remember making $50,000 annual salary and receiving a 4% raise (not much, but actually higher than the average American's raise). This indicates my offense as an engineer produced only $2,000 extra that year. This was a negligible raise, especially when one considers we were starting our family and Laurie was leaving her job. Once inflation and taxes are factored in, this is not a raise at all, and I had to admit my offensive financial plan was anemic.

I was not alone, however, for few people have good offensive financial plans to increase their incomes by $10k, $20k, or even $50k extra over the next few years. In consequence, most financially disciplined people learn to live an "I cannot afford it" lifestyle by living below their means and surrendering their dreams. Indeed, this is why most people *hate* to talk about finances, because they believe it's a depressing plan to surrender dreams by living within one's current income. Thankfully, there is a more palatable financial path.

Whereas many other financial programs focus just on debt reduction, what makes the Financial Fitness and Beyond Financial Fitness Program (FFP) so unique is their dual emphasis on financial defense *and* offense. Don't just live within your means, but also increase the means to live so you can live the life you've always wanted. In this way, a person can still live his dreams and do so debt-free. Instead of just settling for the life you can afford on your present income, why not learn to play offense *and* defense to achieve what you truly want?

This is the fourth and final quadrant of the Financial Matrix, the one where people have both ownership and choices. This group has learned how to play both defense and offense to enjoy a lifestyle that less than 1% in the world can enjoy. These people live below their current means (defense), but also invest heavily in themselves and others (offense). Through building an ongoing income stream (offense), they free themselves from the typical time and money constraints to focus on people and purposes, not merely paychecks or profits. When people decrease expenses and expand skills, their debt decreases while their incomes advance. Compounded over time, this leads to debt-free lifestyles, ownership of assets, and living the life they've always wanted.

Imagine driving dream cars and paying cash; imagine buying dream houses and paying cash or taking dream vacations and again paying cash. Moreover, imagine the causes and charities that can be funded because you broke out of the Financial Matrix debt trap. Far-fetched, impossible, a pipe dream, you say? Then turn the page and read how Laurie and I moved through each of the quadrants on our way to Financial Freedom. We went from being absolutely broke in college (Broke Quadrant), to tightwads and fighting constantly about money (Tightwad Quadrant) after we were married, and finally succumbing to "keeping up with the Joneses" status game (Status Quadrant) before our pregnancy woke us up. The rest is a series of trials and errors as we discovered the right recipe to help people move from the three sub optimal Financial Matrix quadrants to the Financially Free Quadrant.

This book, importantly, isn't just about us. It's also about thousands of others who have chosen a similar path, playing defense and offense as: taught in the FFP, so they can escape the Financial Matrix and live their dreams debt free.

Money is like a sixth sense—and you can't make use of the other five without it.

—WILLIAM SOMERSET MAUGHAM

CHAPTER 2

DEBT IS KILLING THE AMERICAN DREAM

The first thing to understand is that as a person's debt expands, his ability to live his dream contracts. Debt is stealing the proverbial American Dream. While personal debt is bad enough, we must also understand how business debt and government debt are feeding the fiscal crisis. In the first quarter of 2014, the St. Louis Federal Reserve announced the total US debt (the combination of government, business, mortgage, and consumer debt) as nearly $59.4 trillion. That's a boatload of debt! Even at just 5% interest, this amounts to over $3 trillion in interest to service the debt. That's 3,000,000,000,000 dollars every year!

Compare this to the total debt of $2.2 trillion just forty years ago, and it doesn't take a statistician to recognize something has significantly changed in society's treatment of debt. Forty years ago, the total debt was less than the interest paid to service the debt today. The USA debt, unbelievably, has increased more than twenty-seven times in the last forty years! If this doesn't wake someone up to the debt crisis of Western nations, nothing will.

Fortunately, many people are waking up and author James Butler is one of them. He wrote in a recent op-ed piece, "In 50 short years, debt has gone from being a luxury for a few to a convenience for many to an addiction for most to a disease for all. It is a virus that has spread to every aspect of our economy, from a consumer using a credit card to buy a $0.75 candy bar in a vending machine to a government borrowing $17 trillion to keep the lights on."

In other words, households, businesses, and governments (at the local, state, and federal levels) have all been seduced into the web of debt, creating a $59.4 trillion issue. Disastrously, however, it's the people as individuals who end up paying for the debt sins of businesses and governments. Remember, governments do not earn income but rather only receive revenue by taxing their citizens. Thus, when government debt expands (surging past $20 trillion now), the people's taxes must eventually increase to pay the compounding interest due. Has anyone else noticed how much money is taken out of their paychecks in federal, state, and local taxes? Moreover, when Social Security, property taxes, and various licensing fees are added in, it's no wonder most people must borrow in order to live.

Finally, let's not forget about the corporate debt that amounts to nearly $20 trillion in the United States alone. In order to service this debt, corporations increase the price of the products and services they sell. The companies increased debt, in other words, equates to increased prices for consumers. The companies merely combines their corporate taxes, Social Security taxes, and interest on debt into the product costs before adding profit to arrive at the sales price. Shockingly, the already overloaded households are forced to pay, not only for their own financial sins, but also for the corporations' and governments'. Perhaps a visual representation of the Financial

Matrix debt trap will help emphasize the importance of living debt free.

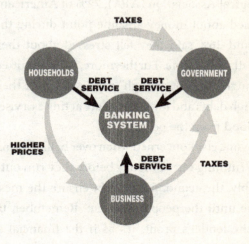

Inflation

Not to belabor the point, but there is still one more factor that undermines the financial solvency of households, namely, inflation. While household incomes are trending downward, inflation is skyrocketing prices upward. We will cover the cause of inflation later, but for now, it's important to recognize that inflation is driving the cost of living through the roof. Yesterday's five-and-dime stores are today's misnamed dollar stores that sell items for ten dollars or more. Increased prices, increased debts and decreased incomes are a deadly combination for any society seeking prosperity. Imagine a nightmare scenario in which people must work sixteen consecutive years for decreasing incomes while prices and taxes continually increase. Now wake up—because this nightmare is real in America right now.

The debt disaster, however, isn't just about math and numbers. Above all else, it's about the massive stress and anxiety it's applying to the families trapped in debt. According to a 2014 study of over 3,000 American adults by the American Psychological Association (APA), 72% of Americans said they felt stressed about money at some point during the previous month, and 26% said they felt stressed about their finances most or all of the time. Furthermore, 54% admitted they had "just enough" or "not enough" money to meet their monthly needs. High debts and low income are acting as a vise squeezing the lifeblood from the people.

Is anyone else concerned when over half of the respondents admit to running out of money before they run out of month? Regrettably, the economics of debt ensure the mess will only get worse until the people wake up. Remember, the people's debt is the lender's profit. It's as if the financial system has changed the old saying, "No pain, no gain" to read "Your pain is our gain" or, more pointedly, "Your pain is our profit." Dismally, the APA survey can be summarized: the banks reap profits by delivering pain.

Society's debt, however, isn't just a story about profits and pain. Control is the key aspect of the debt system. When you view the financial system through the lens of profits and control for the aristocratic elites and subsequent stress and oppression for the masses, you are beginning to see the outlines of the Financial Matrix. Remarkably, the principles of the Financial Matrix are not new. Proverbs 22:7 (NIV) reads, "The rich rule over the poor, and the borrower is slave to the lender." When a person is in debt, he or she is in bondage. Lenders have the power to change the biblical Golden Rule "Do unto others as you would have them do unto you" into a new Golden Rule: "He who has the gold makes the rules."

Curiously, however, the Financial Matrix doesn't coerce people into debt enslavement; instead, it seduces them into it.

Modern marketing campaigns are so effective that many sell themselves into debt by purchasing things they cannot really afford regardless of the "easy" monthly payments.

While many laugh at the humorous (much truth is told in jest) jingle "I owe; I owe; it's off to work I go," it conveys a powerful message. For no one is forced into buying what he or she cannot afford, but once the purchase is made, they are forced to work to pay for it, or risk losing their credit rating and the ability to use credit at all. The alluring ads and seductive slogans cause people to make unwise financial choices they end up paying for over the coming years. Indeed, these high-priced marketing campaigns are specifically designed to make the unreasonable (namely, submit to slavery so you can buy what you cannot afford to own) appear reasonable.

Financial Matrix: Debt System of Control

The Financial Matrix debt system was formed when big governments and big banks killed commodity money and rebooted the monetary system upon paper and digital debt money. As people sell themselves into debt, the Financial Matrix debt system increases its profits and control. As I said earlier, the masses' pain (debt and stress) is the elites' gain (profits and control). To really understand the matrices of control and why the elites create them, a quick history lesson is needed.

For over twenty years, I have researched the political, economic, and social histories of Western civilization, and I have arrived at some startling conclusions. Perhaps the biggest is that the aristocratic elites of every generation created a matrix to exploit the production of the masses. This may sound radical at first, but please bear with me while we place the puzzle pieces together and the full picture comes into view.

My eyes began to open when I read the works of the French political philosopher Bertrand de Jouvenel, who noted (with brackets added by me):

> Whoever does not wish to render history incomprehensible by departmentalizing it—political, economic, social—would perhaps take the view that it is in essence a battle of dominant wills [elites], fighting in every way they can for the material which is common to everything they construct: the human labor force [masses].

In other words, the aristocratic elites (dominant wills) seek methods to control the masses' production (human labor). I certainly saw this control in today's money system, but needed to research this point historically to see if it was true. One of the basic concepts of economics is there are only three factors needed for all production: labor, land, and capital. Indeed, one of the classical economists, John Stuart Mill, wrote, "The Law of the Increase of Production depends on those of Three Elements— Labor, Capital, and Land." When I married these two concepts together (elites seek to control the masses' production and there are only three factors of production), I realized I had discovered the aristocracy's playbook for the matrices of control throughout history, for in order to control the masses' production, the elites must do so by controlling one (or more) of the three factors of production. Now, I needed to determine what the historical record would reveal with respect to the elites and potential matrices of control surrounding labor, land, and capital (money). What I discovered will most likely shock the reader as much as it shocked me.

The aristocracy of each era did, in fact, develop a matrix of control centered upon one of the factors of production. This indicates the Financial Matrix system of control is, in reality, the third matrix of control. The first two were (1) the Physical Matrix and (2) the Feudal Matrix, predictably based upon the other two factors of production. The Physical Matrix is based upon human slavery (an unjust system of control over another person's labor) and is as old as the human records. The Physical Matrix is a straightforward system of control where the "owner" used force to make the other person his property. Then, he claimed the right to the slave's labor (the first factor of production) because he "owned" the slave. Absurd!

The Feudal Matrix, where the aristocracy controlled the serfs by controlling all the land (the second factor of production), was the next matrix of control. Since the serfs needed the land to live, the aristocracy simply captured all the arable domains, forcing the serfs to live on their land and charging the serfs fees in labor and farm produce. Notice how the aristocracy no longer owned the person directly, but rather owned all the land the serfs needed. Thus, they accomplished the same objective—unjust control over the masses' production, by owning the land instead of owning the people. The elites, in other words, did indirectly capture the masses' labor by monopolizing the land (the second factor of production) rather than directly owning the person (the first factor of production).

Thankfully, the Physical Matrix and Feudal Matrix, although not totally eradicated, are much less common today than they were in ancient and medieval history. Nonetheless, this does not mean that today's aristocracy has surrendered its desire to control the masses' labor. On the contrary, it merely indicates the aristocracy has developed a better and subtler system of control—one that focuses on the third factor of all production: capital. Indeed, the Financial Matrix is the greatest form of control yet created by the elites to capture the masses' production because very few people even know it exists, let alone how to stop it.

The Financial Matrix is a system of control where the elites have monopolized the money supply. This allows the modern aristocracy to create money out of thin air to loan to the masses for houses, cars, and other luxuries. Predictably, even though the elites created the money without labor, the masses must then pay back the mortgage over the next 30 years by laboring profusely. In other words, as with the Feudal Matrix, the aristocracy does not own the masses directly but instead controls the masses' labor indirectly by controlling the money supply the masses need in order to live.

The Financial Matrix is the best form of control ever designed by the elites because it is so difficult to detect. Whereas it was easy to see the coercion involved in slavery and serfdom (Physical Matrix and Feudal Matrix, respectively), few people understand that debt money is also coercion and created out of thin air. Think about it. In any history class, the students will learn the historical injustices of slavery and feudalism, but what mainstream high school or college history is teaching the injustices inherent within the modern financial system? Debtors are forced to pay back fiat loans through performing real work. If they don't, invariably, they are coerced into obeisance through threats of litigation, bankruptcy, or shame. The people, although believing themselves free, borrow money from the Financial Matrix to live, then must labor for decades to pay back money created in milliseconds. Unbelievable! While it is unbelievable, it is the truth, and the truth is the only thing that can set someone free.

Although it's not necessary for the reader to understand all the inner workings of the Financial Matrix debt system in order to escape it, some may want a more in-depth analysis of the Financial Matrix system. For the interested reader, I include further discussion on money in the several appendices at the back of the book.

Once we understood the scope of the Financial Matrix, Laurie and I adjusted our financial goals. No longer did we simply want to escape the Financial Matrix personally; we wanted to help others do the same. For just as Edmund Burke is credited with writing, "All that is necessary for the triumph of evil is that good men do nothing," we knew that we must do something. Please don't misunderstand me; it doesn't take a conspiracy for companies to maximize profits, but it does take an education for consumers to minimize pain. In fact, Buckminster Fuller's words describe where our thinking was heading: "You never change things by fighting the existing reality. In order to change something, you need to build a new model that makes the existing one obsolete." Rather than attempting to rally the masses in protest against the existing Financial Matrix, Laurie and I instead focused on educating people on its harmful effects and providing a vehicle for them to escape.

The Truth Shall Set You Free

Interestingly, the very complexity of the Financial Matrix money system is part of its overwhelming success, for the more difficult it is to understand, the less people will comprehend how the system controls them. This reminds me of a scene from the movie The Matrix. If you haven't watched it, I encourage you to do so. Perhaps no other movie has ever captured as much truth in the form of science fiction. The Financial Matrix term, needless to say, is a double entendre, named not only for the graphical 2X2 matrix to display how people respond to it, but also in honor of the movie that revealed how a matrix can control people even when it is not detected.

Remember the scene in which Neo is searching for answers to understand why he feels enslaved even though he lives in an allegededly "free" society? He spends his days working a job and his nights searching for answers to the paradox. Similarly, for over twenty years, I have been building leadership companies as my business and searching for answers in life as my purpose. To me, the discovery of the Financial Matrix system of control is eerily similar to Neo's discovery of the Matrix in the movie. In a particularly telling scene, Morpheus explains to Neo why the world is not as it seems, that the Matrix exists to control the masses' energy (it's a sci-fi thriller, after all) whether they are working, playing, or sleeping. The Matrix is, as Morpheus explains to Neo, "the wool that has been pulled over your eyes to blind you from the truth."[2]

Of course, Neo asks what truth Morpheus is referring to and learns:

That you are a slave, Neo. Like everyone else, you were born into bondage, born into a prison that you cannot smell or taste or touch. A prison…for your mind…. Unfortunately, no one can be…told what the [Financial] Matrix is….You have to see it for yourself.[3]

Morpheus places two pills before Neo and gives him a choice. If he takes the blue pill, Neo will live an illusion and never escape the Matrix. If he takes the red pill, he will learn the truth about the Matrix and how to set himself free.

If you, like Neo, have been searching for answers, the good news is that the search is over. Just as Morpheus offered Neo the chance to learn the truth, so too do I offer you the truth. The rest of the book explains how to escape the Financial Matrix. If you read the book, you will discover how deep the rabbit hole goes and how to escape it. If you don't read the book, you can believe whatever you want to believe locked inside the Financial Matrix. Not to sound overly dramatic, but I truly believe your next move will have long-term financial consequences.

For those moving ahead, it's time to share the billionaire secrets that provided me the roadmap out of the Financial Matrix.

Price is what you pay; Value is what you get.

—WARREN BUFFETT

CHAPTER 3

WARREN BUFFETT'S BILLIONAIRE LESSONS

To achieve financial mastery in life, one of the key decisions people must make is to determine who they are going to listen to. There are two ways to ensure failure: (1) listen to everyone and (2) listen to no one. Personally, I was stuck in the Financial Matrix because everyone I was listening to was also trapped in the Matrix. Doesn't it make sense that people cannot mentor others financially beyond the level of results they themselves have accomplished? To be sure, if people knew how to do better financially, shouldn't they take their own advice before offering it to you? I knew, for instance, that my parents loved me. Nonetheless, it wasn't until I realized they could only give me effective financial advice to the level they had personally achieved that I started changing my financial situation. I made a decision to love and respect my parents but also to stop taking financial advice from them; instead, I sought mentors who had demonstrated the ability to free themselves from the Financial Matrix.

Another key was realizing I had to stop taking my *own* advice. I had heard one of my early mentors say, "If you are not happy with the results you are producing, perhaps it's time to stop taking your own advice." Ouch! That one hurt, but Laurie and I learned our lesson. We started with the end in mind by determining the financial life we wanted and found people who already lived that way. We sought financial wisdom through attending seminars with successful people, and when we couldn't be with them in person, we fed our minds a steady supply of books and audios from the people who had produced or were producing financial results. I believed that if one person could free themselves from the Financial Matrix, then Laurie and I could do so as well by applying the same principles and practices. Warren Buffett's advice that I mentioned earlier was a vital piece of the puzzle to help us change how we thought about money, time, and success.

Warren Buffett's Two Keys to Financial Success

Warren Buffett, in my opinion, is the greatest investment manager of all time. Although he didn't start with much, Buffett implemented disciplined spending habits (minimized expenses) and careful investment strategies (maximized investments) to compound his assets until he became one of the wealthiest people in the world. When Buffett discussed principles on expenses and investments, I was listening. For example, in a CNBC interview in front of an audience of college students, Warren Buffett gave the following advice:

CNBC: *"What is the one thing that young people should be doing about money?"*

Buffett: *"I tell them two things, generally. One is to **stay away from credit cards**...The second thing I tell them is to **invest in themselves**." (Emphasis added.)*

Buffett's short answer contained a ton of wisdom. I separated his advice into two main categories: First, live debt-free (play defense), and second, invest in yourself (play offense). Buffett helped me realize that financial success was not just living like a miser but, rather, both minimizing expenses and also maximizing investments.

In another talk to college students, Buffett emphasized the importance of self-investment. He asked them if they would take $50,000 cash for 10% of their future income. When nearly half the students raised their hands to accept the offer, Buffett pointed out that they must believe they are worth at least $500,000 since 10% of $500,000 is $50,000. He then drove home the message by asking the students how many other $500,000 assets they currently had. Not shockingly, every hand went down. Buffett then concluded by stressing that your number one asset is yourself, so don't be cheap in investing in you. For some reason, I had a hard time with this one before Buffett's reasoning changed me. Sure, if my employer paid for school, I would go, but I didn't understand that I could not rise above my own leadership limitations. If I wanted to grow, then my leadership would have to grow. Buffett made me a believer in financial defense and offense, and it was a game changer for our family.

In yet another interview, Buffett talked about his college diplomas and his certificate from attending a Dale Carnegie public speaking seminar. He told the interviewer that he had no idea where his degrees were, but he proudly displayed his Dale Carnegie certificate behind his desk. Interestingly, Buffett emphasized the importance of reading when he held up stacks of reading materials and stated, "Read 500 pages like this every day. That's how knowledge builds up, like compound interest." If the greatest investment manager in the world believes personal education compounds just like traditional investments, then from then on, I would also be compounding my knowledge. In fact, the Life company was formed to teach Buffett's (and other billionaires') principles to others. FFP, one of our most successful products, teaches people how to eliminate debt. Author Jim Rohn perhaps said it best when he noted, "Formal education will make you a living; self-education will make you a fortune." Once people learn that they are their own greatest asset, they should immerse themselves in financial principles and leadership development and start thinking like billionaires rather than broke people.

Leadership Hard Skills versus Soft Skills

While technical hard skills are typically learned during one's formal education and supplemented with on-the-job training, soft skills are rarely taught in school or at work. Therefore, a potential leader must take personal responsibility for learning and applying the relational soft skills in his or her daily interactions with others. However, to do this properly, one must first understand the difference between a hard skill and a soft skill. Perhaps the simplest method for differentiating between the two types of skills is to consider hard skills as science and soft skills as art. Whereas science focuses on objective numerical outcomes that can be measured, art focuses on subjective aesthetic outcomes that must be experienced. Hard skills (like typing speed, engineering training, IQ level, or computer programming skills) can be measured objectively, while soft

> **Whereas science focuses on objective numerical outcomes that can be measured, art focuses on subjective aesthetic outcomes that must be experienced.**

skills (like teamwork, patience, people skills, public speaking ability, and persistence) can only be measured subjectively.

While most people would think hard skills are more important than soft skills, scientific research reveals just the opposite. For instance, Google, in a study codenamed "Project Oxygen," data-mined every performance review, feedback survey, and nomination for top manager awards within the company. The search engine giant identified the eight most important skills for effective leadership and discovered that technical expertise ranked dead last out of the eight.

Historically, Google's management strategy had been simple: leave the programmers alone and let them reach out to their bosses, who were promoted based upon their mastery of technical skills. However, according to Laszlo Bock, Google's Vice President of "Human Operations," Project Oxygen changed their mindset. "In the Google context, we'd always believed that to be a manager, particularly on the engineering side, you needed to be as deep or deeper a technical expert than the people who work for you," Mr. Bock says. "It turns out that that's absolutely the least important thing. It's important, but pales in comparison. Much more important is just making that connection and being accessible."

Once a person has the basic hard skills, then soft skills become the key differentiator in career advancement and leadership success. Interestingly, Google's findings are not really new but merely confirm statistically what was previously known intuitively, namely, that everything rises and falls on leadership. After all, in 1936, Dale Carnegie wrote, "...15 percent of one's financial success is due to one's technical knowledge and about 85 percent is due to skill in human engineering—to personality and the ability to lead people."

True leaders, in essence, combine the science-side hard skills and the art-side soft skills to build leadership cultures of trust and influence. And every time people invest in themselves, they are building their number one asset. Improved soft skills help people build their most important asset, which improves their earning potential irrespective of whether they are an employee, self-employed, or a business owner.

Buffett taught me the importance of spending less than I make (defense) and investing the difference in assets (offense), beginning with myself. Since everything rises and falls on leadership, Laurie and I realized we needed to grow our leadership abilities in order to grow our business. The only sustainable competitive advantage in today's marketplace is the leadership team's ability to learn faster than the competition.

Expenses versus Investments

Perhaps more than anything else, Buffett taught me the difference between an expense and an investment. Financially speaking, this distinction is what separates the wealthy from the poor. An expense is money spent with no expectation of a return, whereas an investment is money invested for an expected return. Money poured into proper investments produces additional money, while money poured into expenses is simply wasted. Wealthy people maximize investments (in themselves and in business) while minimizing all expenses. In contrast, the poor minimize investments (in themselves and business) while maximizing expenses. In other words, being poor is not so much an income as it is a mindset (and the results of the habits that come from that mindset). One can be poor making $50,000, $100,000, or $200,000 per year. It's not how much a person makes but rather how much goes to investment versus expenses that determines whether one is poor. An investment is anything that will eventually have a return, while an expense is money poured down the drain. The reason Buffett is the greatest investment manager of all time is because he has utilized a higher percentage of his money in investments to compound consistently over time than any other person.

Everyone is familiar with the story of David and Goliath. I like to draw on that story from time to time because it makes for such a universal visual. To succeed at the game of life, people must see life as a series of Goliaths placed in their path to test their faith. When one Goliath is defeated, the victory advances a person up the leadership mountain. The more people exercise their faith, even when they are afraid, the more they become Goliath slayers (achievers) rather than a Goliath circler (procrastinators). Laurie and I were so off-track in our investments and expenses that we knew it was the first Goliath assigned to us to slay.

> **An investment is anything that will eventually have a return, while an expense is money poured down the drain.**

Looking back, it's no wonder we struggled financially. In effect, we did the exact opposite of billionaires with respect to money, expenses, and investments. We maximized entertainment expenses using credit cards, car loans, and same-as-cash impulse buying, and we minimized investments by having no business, no personal development plan, and no tax benefits from having our own business. Either we would change our mindset about money, or we would always lack the funds to invest in ourselves and build a business. Fortunately, we followed through on our commitment to change. First, I tapped into my 401(k) retirement plan to borrow $5,000 from myself in order to start our first business (offense). Second, we cut every expense that wasn't absolutely necessary to live (canceled cable television, sold new cars to drive used, stopped eating out, etc.) and eliminated debt over the next several years.

We were done playing small! We had our long-term dreams: get free from the Financial Matrix and enjoy a better lifestyle without credit of any kind, including home mortgages. And we committed to one another to play defense like champions. In fact, Laurie read the section in Thomas Stanley's book *The Millionaire Next Door* (in which he identifies the wife's spending habits as one of the key factors in wealth accumulation) so many times she could practically repeat it from memory. Because she had long-term dreams, Laurie successfully practiced short-term denials, and today she is enjoying the benefits of our decade of discipline. Whether you choose to play solely defense (a twenty-to-thirty-year plan to get out of the Financial Matrix) or defense *and* offense (generally a two-to-five-year plan out), the important thing is to start today. The sooner you start, the sooner you can change compound interest from working *against* you to working *for* you. The only thing you have to lose is your debt!

Now that we have discussed the importance of eliminating debt (defense) and investing in yourself (offense, part 1), it's time to learn about building a business asset (offense, part 2).

Individuals don't win, Teams do.

—Sam Walton

CHAPTER 4

SAM WALTON: BUILDING BUSINESS ASSETS

Building a business asset is the fastest way to break free from the time-for-money trap. In this chapter, I am going to share what I learned from Sam Walton, the founder of Wal-Mart, about building a business asset. The two keys are:

- Developing people
- Developing turnkey systems

Indeed, when you combine Buffett's financial principles with Walton's business principles, you are developing a plan to break out of the Financial Matrix. When built properly, a business asset produces income through relationships and systems instead of the number of hours or tasks performed.

Unfortunately, few have learned these principles because they are not taught in any traditional educational program. As a matter of fact, only people who have built a business asset are qualified to teach others how to do the same. For this reason, it's time to learn how to build a business asset from one of the most successful businesspeople of the twentieth century and the one I learned from, Sam Walton.

Sam Walton: Building Leaders and Turnkey Business Systems

Today, Wal-Mart is a huge conglomerate of stores across the world, but few remember Sam Walton's "David versus Goliath" historical origins. In 1952, four new entrants joined the discount store market, and three of them were backed by billion-dollar entities: Kmart supported by the Kresge fortune, Woolco supported by Woolworth money, and Target supported by Dayton-Hudson. The fourth new entrant, Wal-Mart, barely had enough money to launch its first store, and the founder himself raised 95% of the money personally. This appeared to be a rigged match, yet somehow Walton won anyway. How was that possible? How did Sam Walton, despite competing in a business model that required massive front-end funding with relative pennies compared to his competitors' dollars, defeat his billionaire foes so convincingly? Whether you admire the Wal-Mart of today is not important, but what is vitally important is to understand how Walton built his business asset in such a manner that it walked over much bigger competitors. To that end, I have read practically everything I could get my hands on about Walton and Wal-Mart to determine what made his business asset so successful. Accordingly, I identified two things that he did better than anyone else, as stated above: build leaders and build turnkey business systems. In reality, every business person must build people and systems, but Walton did both of them better than anyone else.

Developing a Leadership Culture

Sam Walton believed that a successful business must consistently find and build people. He invested significant amounts of time finding the right people, setting high standards for them, and serving them to help everyone—owners, associates, and customers—win. Walton emphasized the importance of leadership when he said, "I needed somebody to run my new store, and I didn't have much money, so I did something I would do for the rest of my run in the retail business without any shame or embarrassment whatsoever: nose around other people's stores searching for good talent." Talent, however, without teamwork can lead to disaster, so Walton encouraged new leaders: "Submerge your own ambitions and help whoever you can in the company. Work together as a team." To build a leadership culture of this caliber, the top leader must focus his or her efforts on serving others.

Once Walton had the right people on the bus and in the right seats, he stressed the importance of communication by saying, "Communicate, communicate, communicate....We do it in so many ways, from the Saturday morning meeting to the very simple phone call to our satellite system. The necessity for good communication in a big company like this is so vital it can't be overstated." Moreover, although he used technology to gather data and communicate his message, he never allowed "high-tech" to replace the people's need for "high-touch." Indeed, Walton emphasized, "A computer is not—and will never be—a substitute for getting out in your stores and learning what's going on. In other words, a computer can tell you down to the dime what you've sold. But it can never tell you how much you could have sold." This was the difference between the managers at his billion-dollar competitors and the leader Walton was. A manager attempts to have high-tech do what only high-touch can do—namely, inspire the human heart to achieve something bigger than itself.

Finally, Walton understood that in order to win consistently in business, the customer must be satisfied. He stated, "Everything we've done since we started Wal-Mart has been devoted to this idea that the customer is our boss...We have never doubted our philosophy that the customer comes ahead of everything else." With the customer satisfied, Walton was then in a position to satisfy his associates who worked with him by developing people and systems. He believed in win-win compensation arrangements to inspire his people to consistently raise the bar on themselves. He wrote, "The more you share profits with your associates—whether it's in salaries or incentives or bonuses or stock discounts—the more profit will accrue to the company. Why? Because the way management treats the associates is exactly how the associates will then treat the customers." Walton created a leadership culture by finding, building, and leading people who bought into his vision of serving his customers. He built a world-class leadership culture that continued to perform impressively after his death. However, what made Wal-Mart capable of defeating Goliath-sized competitors was his marrying of the best leadership culture to the best turnkey business operating system.

Turnkey Business Operations

Impressively, Walton implemented a turnkey business operation that produced superior results as much by predictable systems as with superior people. Indeed, study any billionaire business model, and you will find a turnkey business system producing

> **Successful businesses eliminate chaos by creating predictable processes that lead to successful results.**

repeatable results for anyone who leverages the system. The more predictable the business system, the more predictable the business results. In essence, successful businesses eliminate chaos by creating predictable processes that lead to successful results. Author Michael Gerber explains:

> Once the franchisee learns the system, he is given the key to his own business. Thus, the name: Turn-Key Operation. The franchisee is licensed the right to use the system, learns how to run it, and then "turns the key." The business does the rest. And the franchisees love it! Because if the franchisor has designed the business well, every problem has been thought through. All that's left for the franchisee to do is learn how to manage the system.

Sam Walton separated himself from the crowd by not just building a business but by building a business system that produced results even when he was sleeping.

Abe Marks, the first president of National Mass Retailers' Institute (NMRI) trade association, described Walton's business philosophy:

> He knew that he was already in what the trade calls an "absentee ownership" situation. That just means you're putting your stores out where you, as management, aren't. If he wanted to grow he had to learn to control it. So to service these stores you've got to have timely information: How much merchandise is in the store? What is it? What's selling and what's not? What is to be ordered, marked down, and replaced?

The Information Age has further allowed turnkey operations to blossom because one can study data from each store on a real-time basis. Marks, again, explained why this was crucial for Walton:

> He was really ten years away (in 1966) from the computer world coming. But he was preparing himself. And this is an important point: without the computer, Sam Walton could not have done what he's done. He could not have built a retailing empire the size of what he's built, the way he built it. He's done a lot of other things right, too, but he could not have done it without the computer. It would have been impossible.

Walton studied the data from each store to ensure the targets he set were being hit. In effect, he inspected what he expected. Walton described his process:

> That's why I come in every Saturday morning usually around two or three [a.m.], and go through all the weekly numbers. I steal a march on everybody else for the Saturday morning meeting. I can go through those sheets and look at a store, and even though I haven't been there in a while, I can remind myself of something about it, the manager maybe, and then I can remember later that they are doing this much business this week and that their wage cost is such and such. I do this with each store every Saturday morning. It usually takes about three hours, but when I'm done I have as good a feel for what's going on in the company as anybody here—maybe better on some days.

All of this pinpoints one of Walton's key business principles: build a business system that can work anywhere whether the owner is present or not. Billionaire businesses build systems that work without the owner's long-term involvement. For me personally, this was an entirely different way of looking at business and life, for up to that point, I had always focused on how hard I could work rather than how good a system I could develop. Interestingly, I had been formally trained as a systems engineer, but I had never thought to apply the concept to my personal financial life!

Today, the Internet has leveled the business playing field. Anyone with an entrepreneurial spirit can start a business, building people and a turnkey business system from home. Moreover, people can track their progress by studying real-time data from their home computer.

Billionaires build leaders to orchestrate duplicatable systems to accomplish work. In contrast, the majority of people do not build themselves or systems; thus, they are the system that is worked. Indeed, Walton's leadership culture and turnkey business systems were so effective that the business didn't miss a beat after his death. This was possible because he created a business asset that included a top-notch leadership team and a top-notch system.

These are the essential minimums to succeed in building a business asset that outlasts your efforts. Walton's example inspired me to do the same, namely, build leaders and build systems that would work whether I was working that day or not. Now that I understood Buffett's and Walton's key principles of success, I was ready for the third key lesson.

*Billionaires' working hours are twenty-four seven.
They don't wait till Monday.*

—Sophie Page

CHAPTER 5

BILLIONAIRE SECRETS TO WEALTH

The final piece of the billionaire business puzzle developed from studying the biographies and autobiographies of hundreds of billionaires. Without exaggeration, I read thousands of books to cull the three principles every billionaire used to create his or her wealth. The three Billionaire Secrets to Wealth are:

1. Long-Term Dreams
2. Short-Term Denials
3. Long-Term Duplication

No matter whose story I read, it quickly became apparent that every billionaire used similar principles to achieve massive success with time. It didn't matter which particular field each billionaire chose to focus on (whether automobiles, computers, or even makeup); the underlying principles were still applied consistently, as we saw with Buffett and Walton. As a result, Buffett, Walton, and the rest of the billionaires inspired me to apply my manufacturing systems training to build a business rather than work a job.

Along the way, I finally understood why Laurie and I were stuck in the Financial Matrix for so long. In effect, we violated every one of the financial principles. We didn't have a long-term financial plan to guide our decision making; we didn't practice short-term denials because our emotions consistently trumped our logic; and finally, we had compound interest leveraged against us rather than in our favor. We realized that when we went to sleep at night, the compound interest didn't. Consequently, we woke up every day more broke than we were the night before. How demoralizing.

> **The Bible says the truth will set you free, but this is usually the case only after the truth ticks you off.**

The Bible says the truth will set you free (John 8:32, NIV), but this is usually the case only after the truth ticks you off. I was ticked, but I was also excited because the plan to escape our Financial Matrix was coming together. Laurie and I committed to making the needed changes. I knew in my heart that the billionaires were no better than we were, but they had applied better principles. However, if we did what they did, then we could live as they lived.

> **If we did what they did, then we could live as they lived.**

The Mentors and the Plan

After my business partners and I studied the Billionaire Secrets to Wealth and the financial challenges of people in the developed world, the Life business plan practically wrote itself. Life is about setting people free at three levels as the graph below conveys. Life is an information-based company that supports all three groups with cutting-edge materials and services.

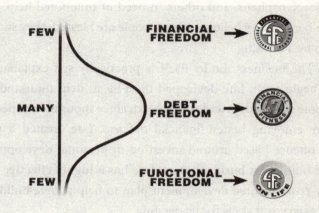

For some, it's about financial freedom and living their dreams. For many others, it's about playing defense and getting debt-free to live without the stress and anxiety debt causes. Finally, for the last group, it's about getting help to be functionally free.

Shockingly, it's estimated that over 21% of Americans cannot read at a fifth grade level. This is dangerous for all of the freedoms in society when nearly a quarter of its members cannot read for themselves. But we believed we could play a part in helping free the minds of people who are trapped by their inability to read, learn, grow, and change.

Thus, we created the Life on Life Initiative, which Life funds to promote literacy. Furthermore, Life corporate offices also provide weekly paid absences for employees who volunteer time to help adolescents and adults learn to read. Another method by which Life supports functional freedom is through giving 100% of its corporate profits from the All Grace Outreach (AGO) subscription to the AGO foundation. This, along with thousands of individual donations from Life members helps AGO give to numerous charities that serve widows, orphans, and others in need of functional help. The Life community believes when people are blessed, they should also be a blessing.

The business model itself is practically self-explanatory. To begin with, Life developed the FFP to help thousands of people reduce debt and stress. Next, since thousands of people were enjoying better financial defense, Life created a plan for offense based around investing in personal development and building a business asset. Life has a highly effective and low-cost personal development plan to help people build the necessary soft skills for leadership.

Meanwhile, Life developed a turnkey marketing system to help people build a business asset by sharing the FFP information with others. We thought: Why not create a business asset that helps people learn financial literacy (defense, offense, and playing field of finances) and rewards people for modeling financial literacy and sharing the message of financial literacy with others? Life's Compensated Community leverages the billionaire principles (minimize expenses, maximize investments, and build a business asset) to help people stuck in the Financial Matrix develop a plan to escape. Already, Life has helped many people escape the Financial Matrix entirely, while many more are on their way to debt-free living.

Finally, why not compensate people in a fair and equitable manner for spreading the financial message to the world? The monthly compensation can vary for people between a few dollars to tens of thousands of dollars, based on their goals, efforts, and results. (See the Life Compensation Plan Brochure and Income Disclosure Statement for further details.) Many join the Compensated Community in order to have an accountability group to keep themselves disciplined and committed to their new financial plan (defense). Others, however, are applying both the defense and the offense by building large and profitable Compensated Communities. People choose their own commitment level based on the results they desire. Indeed, Life isn't just a business built on purpose; it's actually our purpose built on a business. The Life founders apply the principles we teach. We were each stuck in the Financial Matrix just like nearly everyone else. Fortunately, however, through practicing the principles learned from the billionaires and shared in the FFP, the Life founders were able to break out of the Financial Matrix.

After we confirmed we had an accurate roadmap out of the Financial Matrix, the founders created Life to share the roadmap with others. Instead of protesting injustices by occupying streets or attending tea parties (although both sides have valid points, the historical record of peasant protest is extremely poor), we believe the best way to protest is non-participation in the Financial Matrix. This marries the ideas of personal responsibility and the application of the billionaire principles to create a business based on "conscientious objection"; our consciences object to participating in the Financial Matrix any longer!

This is the core teaching of Life: Consistently spend less than you make and invest the difference in yourself (Buffett's two financial secrets). Then build a turnkey business system by sharing the financial principles with others to produce wealth and freedom outside the Financial Matrix.

Now that you are familiar with Buffett's and Walton's principles, it's time to learn how Life applies the Billionaire Secrets to Wealth (long-term dreams, short-term denials, and long-term duplication) so you can utilize these principles to live the life you've always wanted by losing the debt you've never needed.

You are never too old to set another goal or to dream a new dream.

—C.S. LEWIS

CHAPTER 6

LONG-TERM DREAMS

Still, in order to *live the life you've always wanted*, you're probably going to have to face some things you've always avoided. Essentially, a person's circumstances will not change until the person does. This is where long-term dreams come into play. People cannot change their future until they have the courage to envision it. After all, a dream is just tomorrow's reality expressed as an idea today. And only when people see the dream in their mind are they capable of

> **In order to *live the life you've always wanted*, you're probably going to have to face some things you've always avoided.**

bringing it into reality. In other words, the dream must come before the action. Unfortunately, few people have a long-term financial dream. Instead, most people are like sailboats without a rudder, merely blown in the financial wind. Laurie and I knew that our long-term dream was bigger than just being job-optional. We wanted total independence from the Financial Matrix debt system without having to live like paupers.

In a similar fashion, it is necessary to invest the time to express this long-term dream as an idea today. As my good friend and cofounder of Life Bill Lewis says, "It's not how big you dream; it's how long you dream big." Success, in a sense, is a picture in the mind's eye that you maintain no matter what. What success picture do you have the courage to imagine? Once a person eliminates debt, his or her money begins to accumulate quickly, so he or she should not delay in cultivating a dream for the future. Regrettably, many people think the choice is between debt and their dreams because they cannot imagine how they could wipe out their debt and still have enough money to live their dreams. But this is exactly what long-term dreaming is about.

Dreams do come true for those who are true to their dreams. The first part of being true to a dream is expressing it verbally because the long-term dream is defining the life a person desires once time and money are no longer constraints. To be sure, achieving dreams demands time and sacrifice, but that is why they're called long-term dreams. A person cannot fix in months what has taken years to mess up. All real change must first begin with a change in *thinking*.

> **Dreams do come true for those who are true to their dreams.**

To change our finances, Laurie and I knew we had to change the way we thought about money, time, and wealth creation. This is why Buffett's advice was so important to us. We need not only financial defense (to minimize expenses) but also financial offense (to maximize investments). In today's microwave world, a decade may seem like an eternity, but in reality, time passes quickly. Do you remember where you were when the Twin Towers fell? I certainly do. I received a phone call from my good friend Chris Brady in time to turn on my rarely-used television and see them come down. I was practically in a state of shock. Defining moments like this are rarely forgotten and are remembered vividly as if they happened yesterday. But it's almost unbelievable that that all happened fourteen years ago! Like I said, time flies regardless of what we do with it along the way.

Realize that a decade is going to go by whether you develop a long-term dream or not. However, your financial results will be much different depending upon the choices you make during that decade. Laurie and I committed to a decade of discipline in order to radically change our finances. Inexorably, the decade has come and gone, but the discipline has changed everything. We applied the three Billionaire Secrets to Wealth consistently, and by late 2004 (ten years to the day later), we paid off the mortgage on our dream home. We were officially free from the Financial Matrix. Better yet, we have not borrowed any money since then. I am not saying this to shed light on us, but rather to illuminate the effectiveness of the principles taught in the FFP. The principles work. The only question is whether you will discipline yourself to apply them. Thankfully, this is made much easier by associating with others in the Life community who are also applying the defensive and offensive principles consistently in order to break free from the Financial Matrix. As the Bible says, "Iron sharpens iron" (Proverbs 27:17, NIV).

There are several questions to answer in developing a long-term financial dream. First, if you knew your dream couldn't fail, what would it include? Needless to say, your dream should include more than just material things (houses, cars, and toys). It should also involve the type of person you want to become, the type of friends you want to associate with, and the legacy you intend to leave. Your long-term dream, in effect, should be the successful realization of your "tombstone test." This is where you see yourself at your funeral and imagine what people will say about your life and work. Once you know your long-term dream, you can then identify the proper roadmap to take you from your present reality to your future dream.

The Ant and the Elephant

Author Jack Canfield writes that you have control over only three things in life: "the thoughts you think, the images you visualize, and the action you take." Since the conscious mind thinks in words, while the subconscious mind thinks in images, few people realize the subconscious mind is actually much more powerful than the conscious one. Olympian Vince Poscente, for example, termed the two minds "the ant and the elephant." He explained that the conscious (ant) mind stimulates 2,000 neurons per second while the subconscious (elephant) mind stimulates four billion neurons per second. In other words, the subconscious mind is two million times more powerful in programming the brain than is the conscious mind. Researcher Erik Colonies elaborates:

> Scientists are discovering that the brain is a visionary device, the primary function of which is to create pictures in our minds that can be used as blueprints for things that don't exist. They are also learning that our brains can work subconsciously to solve problems that we cannot crack through conscious reasoning, and that the brain is a relentless pattern seeker, constantly reinventing the world.

To accomplish a long-term dream, you must learn to program your subconscious mind with positive images of your future life. As Albert Einstein once stated, "Imagination is everything. It is the preview of life's coming attractions."

Please don't misunderstand me; I'm not suggesting sitting on the sofa all day and visualizing your future will mysteriously make all your dreams come true. Rather, it's the alignment of the logical mind (Ant) and emotional mind (Elephant) married to hard work that achieves big-time results. As Olympian Peter Vidmar stressed: "Visualization is not a substitute for hard work and dedication. But if you add it to your training regimen—whether in sports, business, or your personal relationships—you will prepare your mind for success, which is the first step in achieving all your goals and dreams." My good friend Rob Robson, for instance, changed himself from the inside out by going on a media fast to cleanse himself from the negative thoughts holding him back. He replaced his TV, radio, and magazines with inspiring audios, books, and seminars, and today, he and his lovely wife, Kenyon own one of the most profitable Life businesses. Success starts with a proper vision, then it is backed up by consistent effort. Historian Eugene Ferguson noted similarly when he wrote:

> Pyramids, cathedrals, and rockets exist not because of geometry, theory of structures, or thermodynamics, but because they were first pictures—literally visions—in the minds of those who first conceived them. Usually the significant governing decisions regarding an artisan's or an engineer's design have been made before the artisan picks up tools or the engineer turns to his drawing board.

While most people say they have to see to believe, achievers actually believe to see. A dream, again, is first seeing in the mind and then acting in the world to make the dream a reality. Dr. Maxwell Maltz emphasized, "The goals that the Creative Mechanism seek to achieve are MENTAL IMAGES or mental pictures, which we create by the use of IMAGINATION." Achievers imagine so vividly that it is experienced as real, leading Maltz to conclude, "Clinical psychologists have proven beyond a shadow of a doubt that the human nervous system cannot tell the difference between an actual experience and an experience imagined vividly and in detail." When you understand the power of belief, you are on the verge of moving any mountains standing in your way.

In 1987, for example, a struggling actor who couldn't even afford to pay his bills drove his old Toyota up Mulholland Drive into the Hollywood Hills. As he stared down at the City of Angels, he imagined his future in vivid detail. By feeding his subconscious mind the long-term dreams he imagined, this young actor experienced feelings as if they were real even though they were only imagined in his mind. Before he left, he wrote himself a check, dated for Thanksgiving Day, 1995, "for acting services rendered," in the amount of ten million dollars. To practically everyone else, this action would have seemed absurd, for only the upper echelon actors ever make that type of compensation. Jim Carrey's subconscious, however, experienced the event as real, and years later it was real. In fact, Jim Carrey has surpassed twenty million dollars for acting services rendered. If anything, he didn't dream big enough! Actor Jim Carrey consistently fed his elephant mind the future he envisioned and accomplished what author Claude Bristol describes: "This subtle force of repeated suggestion overcomes our reason. It acts directly on our emotions and our feelings, and finally penetrates to the very depths of our subconscious minds. It's the repeated suggestion that makes you believe."

Financial Matrix Quadrants: Ant and Elephant

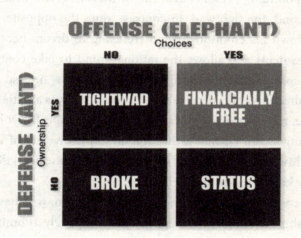

Unfortunately, despite the research and popular books, few people have any idea how important it is to learn how to align the Ant and the Elephant mind. Instead, their minds are in a state of constant turmoil, a civil war brewing between the logical mind and the emotional mind, a battle that destroys all hope for united mental action. Of course, without mental alignment, the person burns all his energy in internal battles and has little time or energy left for the external battles necessary for success in any field. This is success suicide, for every high achiever must utilize his logical and emotional mind to move ahead.

Not surprisingly, three out of the four quadrants in the Financial Matrix suboptimize success because they do not align their Ant and Elephant minds. First, the status seeker shuts down the logical mind (refusing to ponder how foolish it is to subjugate himself to debt merely for a temporary buzz of an emotional purchase) and allows the emotional mind to take charge. As a result, the status person experiences the short-term joy of pretend dreams (choices) and the long-term pain of compounding personal debt (no ownership). How insane!

Second, the tightwad, in contrast, does the opposite. He shuts down his emotional mind (refusing to dream because he hates debt) and allows the rational mind to take control. While commendably owning most of his assets, he also has rationalized away his dreams (no choices) and lives a settle-for lifestyle, resisting anyone or anything that attempts to get him dreaming again. Dismally, through an impressive act of will, the tightwad forces himself to live below his means, killing debt by killing his dreams. How sad!

The worst case, however, is the broke person, who has no ownership or choices. Indeed, he has completely submitted himself to the Financial Matrix debt system, the Ant and Elephant minds disengaged from reality while debts increase and dreams decrease. The 50% of Americans who are broke have surrendered their dreams, no longer being grown-up dreamers but now given-up debtors. Debt has crushed their ability to think, so they simply work to pay bills to survive another day. How inhuman!

Needless to say, none of these quadrants allow people to live their dreams because they haven't aligned the Ant and the Elephant to end the mental civil war. This is what makes the Financially Free quadrant so unique. It is the only one where people have ended the civil war to get both the conscious (defense) and subconscious (offense) working together financially to achieve financial success. The people in this quadrant enjoy both the ownership of assets and the liberty of choices because they use the rational mind to budget today's expenses while applying the emotional mind to dream bigger for tomorrow. How liberating!

How does a person become Financial Free? It begins with understanding how the Financial Matrix debt system is enslaving people, learning to play defense (applying the logical Ant mind to develop a financial plan) and finally learning to play offense (applying the emotional Elephant mind to dream). This is how Laurie and I, starting with few skills, money, or time, built the life we always wanted. Although certainly this wasn't easy in the beginning, failing financially isn't easy in the beginning, the middle, or the end. What did we do? Well, in a nutshell, we ended the civil war, aligning our Ant and Elephant minds through reading, listening, and associating with other successful people who had terminated their mental civil war. Then we took massive action!

Action: Where the Rubber Meets the Road

Now that we have the dream right, it's time to get the actions right. Financial success demands excellent defense and offense to outrun the Financial Matrix. Success is hard work, but failure is hard also and lasts longer. As part of Life's turnkey marketing system, we studied many people who successfully escaped the Financial Matrix to determine what behaviors they practiced in common. The behaviors fell into four main areas, some of which I have mentioned previously:

- Read
- Listen
- Associate
- Apply

These four practices help people move from an employee/ self-employed mindset to a turnkey business owner mindset. For that reason, Life created the Power Player program to help people combine the right process with the right actions. The Power Player program combines each of these four steps into an organized program that is both fun and rewarding to follow. Such a program makes it easier to acquire the new habits necessary for success that often come disguised simply as hard work. Indeed, hard work combined with a few improvements (through mentorship and studying other successful people) compounded over 10,000 hours helps people develop mastery.

Interestingly, most people believe mastery is a matter of talent rather than discipline, but researcher K. Anders Ericsson proved otherwise. Indeed, he chose a field that has traditionally been assumed to be filled with naturally talented individuals: the music industry. Certainly, if any field could prove that hard work alone cannot produce mastery; it would be the musical profession. However, author Malcolm Gladwell described how Ericsson's study proved the exact opposite. The striking thing about Ericsson's study is that he and his colleagues couldn't find any "naturals," musicians who floated effortlessly to the top while practicing a fraction of the time their peers did. Nor could they find any "grinds," people who worked harder than everyone else yet just didn't have what it took to break into the top ranks. Their research suggests that once a musician has enough ability to get into a top music school, the thing that distinguishes one performer from another is how hard he or she works. That's it. And what's more, the people at the very top don't just work harder or even much harder than everyone else. They work much, much harder.

Mastery, as the research has proven, has little to do with talent. Practically everyone has enough talent, but few seem willing to do the hard work combined with the daily improvements compounded over 10,000 hours. I was excited when I read Ericsson's research because I never felt I had much talent, but I knew I could work hard and do so consistently. Still, it isn't just 10,000 hours, for many have worked the hours without achieving mastery. Rather, it's 10,000 hours with proper coaching and course-correcting. Otherwise, someone may believe he or she has 10,000 hours of experience when he or she actually has an hour's experience repeated 10,000 times. Author Geoff Colvin called this constant improvement mindset "deliberate practice" and wrote:

> Deliberate practice is characterized by several elements, each worth examining. It is activity designed specifically to improve performance, often with a teacher's help; it can be repeated a lot; feedback on results is continuously available; it's highly demanding mentally, whether the activity is purely intellectual, such as chess or business-related activities, or heavily physical, such as sports; and it isn't much fun.

Deliberate practice, in effect, separates the amateurs from the professionals in every field. Amateurs typically practice in their comfort zone on skills they have already mastered, while professionals work in the uncomfortable zone to expand their range of skill mastery. Abraham Lincoln modeled this attitude when he said, "I will work, I will study, and when my moment comes, I will be ready."

Anyone can master the skills of wealth building, but

Deliberate practice separates the amateurs from the professionals in every field.

unless a person is locked into his or her long-term dreams, he or she will not persist in the uncomfortable zone to develop mastery. Achievers, in a sense, learn to become comfortable being uncomfortable. This is what is needed for mastery. Perhaps Professor Robert Grudin described it best:

> The process of achieving their professional level is usually full of pain. Such mastery demands endless practice of technical operations, endless assaults on seemingly ineluctable concepts, humiliation by teachers, anxious and exhausting competition with peers. To gain such mastery, one must face the sting of pertinent criticism, the shock of a thousand minor failures, and the nagging fear of one's own unimprovable inadequacy.

Achievers hate losing enough to change, while the rest hate changing enough to lose.

So why do achievers do it? Because they hate losing enough to change, while the rest hate changing enough to lose. Achievers endure the pain to receive the gain, while non-achievers skip the pain and the gain. Movie star Will Smith stressed his work ethic when he stated:

> I'm not afraid to die on a treadmill. I will not be outworked. You may be more talented than me. You might be smarter than me. And you may be better looking than me. But if we get on a treadmill together you are going to get off first or I'm going to die. It's really that simple. I'm not going to be outworked.

Long-term dreams, in sum, lead to hard work, which leads to persistence. As Vince Lombardi once proclaimed, "The harder you work, the harder it is to surrender."

Bill Lewis: Long-Term Dreams

Bill Lewis grew up in the inner city of Saginaw, Michigan. Unlike most of his acquaintances, however, he had a dream. His lack of capital forced him to work in a job he didn't necessarily love in order to live. Bill launched several entrepreneurial ventures (vending machines and rental properties, to name a couple) in an effort to fulfill his dreams, but none of them lived up to their advance billing. As a result, he found himself increasing his debt and decreasing his opportunities to escape his rut.

This is where most people would give up, but Bill is not like most people. In spite of his setbacks, he refused to surrender his dream to be free, and when a coworker shared with him a plan for breaking free from the Financial Matrix, he was ready. He started with a steady diet of books, audios, and seminars to help him develop a better attitude and mindset. In the process, he filled his subconscious mind with the future he desired and didn't let his current reality overcome his future dream. Despite massive financial and emotional stress, Bill kept his eyes on the prize of financial freedom and refused to lose. He knew what he wanted, and no criticism from friends, family, or coworkers was going to stop him from achieving his dream. And with the help of his mentors and teammates, Bill was able to achieve a debt-free lifestyle in just less than three years. Along the way, he met the girl of his dreams, Jackie, and they had four amazing children together. Sadly, after eleven years of marital bliss, tragedy struck, and Jackie was hospitalized and eventually passed away from liver and kidney failure. As

Bill spent the next year grieving his loss with his children, his business continued to provide an income for him and his family. In fact, Bill's community actually grew as his team rallied to help him the only way they knew how: by growing personally and professionally.

Perhaps Bill's best trait is his resilience, and it was never more on display than after Jackie's passing. Indeed, there are few people I know who have dealt with and overcome as many challenges as Bill Lewis. He has learned to make lemonade out of life's lemons. This is why having a long-term dream is so important, for challenges are a given, but overcoming is just an option. Sadly, most people choose to sell their dreams to buy their excuses instead of choosing to sell their excuses to buy their dreams. Bill had plenty of excuses, but he used them as reasons to build a business asset.

Eventually, Bill met another amazing woman, Keisha, and married her, combining his four children with her four to build a new family. Today, the Lewis family enjoys living in a beautiful 8,300-square-foot home in Grand Blanc, Michigan, and Bill is one of the founders of Life. He is living proof that long-term dreams do have the power to change a person's destiny.

This would be a much better world if more married couples were as deeply in love as they are in debt.

—EARL WILSON

CHAPTER 7

SHORT-TERM DENIALS

Once they have long-term dreams, a dream to be Financially Free with ownership and choices, people are ready to implement the second principle every billionaire practices: short-term denials. Learning to deny the urge for instant gratification by focusing on long-term dreams is essential for success in any field. Short-term denial is the ability to resist an immediate smaller reward and build instead for a larger, more enduring one. While most acknowledge this to be a good principle, few seem to live it.

> **Short-term denial is the ability to resist an immediate smaller reward and build instead for a larger, more enduring reward.**

The reason why becomes clear when one remembers that marketers and advertisers receive big money to get people to buy on impulse rather than on logic. This returns us to the discussion on the conscious (Ant) mind and the subconscious (Elephant) mind. In order to deny gratification in the short term, a person must program his Elephant subconscious with the long-term dream he desires. This is vital, for without this step, the marketers will fabricate dreams using their products to replace the mental void caused by a person not dreaming for himself. Marketers are experts at exciting the bored subconscious mind (Elephant) to charge off in the direction of counterfeit dreams with debt! Therefore, the real question is: Who is programming your subconscious Elephant? The answer, based upon how few people practice short-term denials, is the marketers who are doing most of your mental programming. This must end if you are to be financially successful.

Perhaps the best place to start is to limit the amount of television exposure. Indeed, the average person consumes around four to five hours of television and media per day. Therefore, the subconscious mind of most people is deluged with images designed to get them to emotionally buy what they cannot afford. Author Erik Calonius noted the impact such repeated image exposures have on the mind: "The researchers found that the subjects like the pictures they had already seen. Researchers call this the 'mere exposure effect.' That's why advertisers pound ads repeatedly down our throats. It's why chain restaurants (you get the same meal coast to coast) thrive."

Not surprisingly, successful advertisers ignore the conscious (Ant) mind and instead focus on the subconscious (Elephant) mind, creating an Elephant charge by feeding the subconscious a steady diet of seductive images. Advertisers have learned from experience that providing a list of functions, features, and benefits to the Ant mind doesn't produce nearly the results that feeding alluring images to the Elephant mind does. Philosopher Dan Dennett describes the subconscious mind as the "President," while the conscious mind is just its "Press Secretary." Advertisements encourage the "President" to buy things on emotion that aren't truly needed while the "Press Secretary" creates a rational reason for the irrational purchase. High-paid marketers, in a nutshell, promise the masses happiness by feeding manufactured images to their subconscious minds. This elicits an unwise purchasing decision by the multitude, which increases profits for companies and pain for people.

Be that as it may, if advertisers seduce our subconscious minds into the Financial Matrix trap, then people can program their own subconscious mind to escape it. Once I understood that the Elephant mind merely charges toward the images it is consistently fed, Laurie and I began to control what was fed to our Elephant minds. This is one of the keys to freedom from the Financial Matrix: refusing to be seduced into buying things we cannot afford. Once people assume responsibility for feeding their Elephant mind, they are moving toward their long-term dreams. As Maxwell Maltz explains, "We act, or fail to act, not because of the will, as is so commonly believed, but because of imagination. A human being always acts and feels and performs in accordance with what he imagines to be true about himself and his environment."

Remember the verse in Luke that reads, "He that is faithful in that which is least is faithful also in much: and he that is unjust in the least is unjust also in much" (Luke 16:10, KJV)? This is one of the key ingredients to financial success. The FFP teaches people how to be faithful in their current income, so that they have seed money to invest in themselves and their future. Essentially, if people cannot manage their current income, they will prove unfaithful even when or if they make more. For instance, how many stories have we heard about how lottery winners made and lost millions of dollars, eventually being forced to declare bankruptcy? How is this possible? Simply stated, without a solid financial education, making more money can be dangerous. Indeed, banks and credit cards provide more credit to people with higher incomes, basically providing the rope for financially illiterate people to hang themselves.

Fortunately, regardless of a person's income level, the FFP teaches specific defensive principles to help them spend less than they make monthly. Moreover, Life offers Financial Fitness Services that allows people to track all expenses and save at thousands of national and local vendors. Be sure to check out the many testimonials of people who have eliminated debt and saved money using the Financial Fitness Services on the Life website (mainhomepage.com). Playing defense, in other words, is vital to restoring financial liberty. For only when people enjoy financial freedom by building a business asset without debt are they truly free from the Financial Matrix.

Robert Kiyosaki created the CASHFLOW Quadrant to identify and explain the four ways people go on offense to create cash flow. Each of the four quadrants represents a category of income generation: Employee, Self-Employed, Business Owner, and Investor.

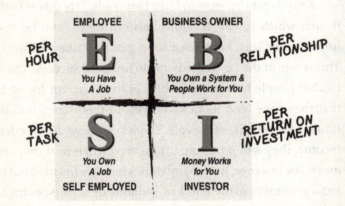

Each of them has pros and cons that must be considered when choosing which quadrant to work within. Every reader is in one, or more, of these quadrants, and it's important to understand how to move from one's current quadrant into the Business and Investor quadrants in order to escape the Financial Matrix. In truth, it doesn't matter which quadrant people start in so long as they apply Long-Term Dreams, Short-Term Denials, and Long-Term Duplication to move themselves into the Business and Investor quadrants. The important principle is to live below your current income to generate the seed money to invest in your business asset and harvest your financial freedom.

Employee Quadrant: "Per Hour" Pros and Cons

Repeat after me: "If you want to be successful, you need to get good grades and get a good job with benefits, and then you can live the American Dream." Anyone ever hear that one growing up? I heard that hundreds of times growing up. A good job, in reality, does provide a high level of security (at least in a good economy) since employees receive income whether or not they (or the company) were productive that month. Employees, in short, get paid per hour sold. This leads to predictable levels of income and an easier path with which to develop a solid defensive financial plan. If, however, a person's income varies month to month, it becomes difficult to build an effective defensive plan. Above everything else is the little downside risk if the company fails. In this case, an employee merely gets another job, while the entrepreneur who started a traditional brick-and-mortar business is typically still responsible for paying back creditors. Indeed, if the business owner cannot handle the debt load, he or she will end up in bankruptcy proceedings. The Employee quadrant, in sum, is a great short-term place for people to start their journey to the Business and Investor quadrants since it provides a steady stream of income. The predictable income allows people to live below their means and to invest the difference into building a business to free themselves from the Financial Matrix.

However, employees who choose to remain employees must also recognize the risk associated with this choice. First, for any people who consider themselves to be hungry, honeable, and honorable, the upside rewards in a job environment are minimal. Pay raises are typically distributed within a small range regardless of each individual's personal contribution. At most, a high achiever may make 5–10% more than the average even though he or she may be contributing ten times more to the company's bottom line. Long-term employees, in essence, follow a forty-five-year plan in which incomes level off around twenty-five years of age, and raises barely keep up with the cost of living afterward. This flat line continues until retirement, when the employees are then forced to make it on 50% or less of the income they already thought wasn't enough when they were working full-time.

Interestingly, when I learned about the employee forty-five-year plan, I was twenty-six years old. I remember sitting down with my dad to graph it out for him. I showed him how employees pay flat-lined from around age twenty-five until age sixty-five and told him this wasn't working for me. His response, as a sixty-year-old retired electrician, was classic: "You know what, son? It didn't work for me either! I'm making less than half in retirement of what I made working full-time." Sure, this is funny today, but it wasn't when I first heard it! Later, I learned that a person must take advice from someone who has escaped the Financial Matrix, for how can a person trapped in the Financial Matrix teach someone else how to escape? My mom and dad gave me the best advice they knew, but they did not know how to escape the Financial Matrix and thus could not teach me how to either. I had to admit that I had spent eight years of my life climbing a ladder that could not take me where I wanted to go. If the definition of insanity is continuing to do the same thing while expecting a different result, then I was flirting with insanity.

The 45 Year Plan

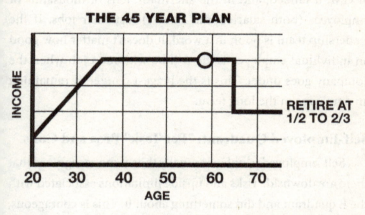

THE 45 YEAR PLAN

INCOME

RETIRE AT
1/2 TO 2/3

20 30 40 50 60 70
AGE

Above all, what leads most people out of the E quadrant is when they realize they are at the mercy of the company's leadership for their security and advancement. For example, when I resigned from AC Rochester to start my own consulting company, many told me it was risky. Nevertheless, I felt it was riskier to rely on the company's management for my economic future rather than on my own performance. For the management team's poor decision didn't just affect them, but everyone else's income regardless of their personal performance. This is exactly what occurred at our division. The growth had slowed due to bad leadership, and as a twenty-five year old seventh-level engineer, I was notified that they wouldn't consider promoting me to eighth level (a much sought-after level of distinction with perks like a company car within the enormous General Motors hierarchy) until I was 32. The reason for this disappointing news was because the division was going backward, and with decreasing revenues, they didn't have any spots open regardless of one's performance. Seven years of hard work with no chance for promotion seemed ludicrous to me. Strangely, to most of the engineers, it didn't. After AC Rochester became independent of GM, it tanked, and in the aftermath, tens of thousands of employees (both salaried and hourly) lost their jobs. If the leadership team is poor, in a word, it doesn't matter how good an individual employee is, he will be without a job when the company goes under. This is the biggest danger of remaining an employee in the long term.

Self-Employed Quadrant: "Per Task" Pros and Cons

Self-employed people are usually those who recognized that there are downside risks and upside limitations associated with the E quadrant and did something about it. This is courageous, and S quadrant income earners ought to be commended for making the entrepreneurial leap. A large benefit of a self-employed business situation is the greater level of control people have over their business and income potential. Self-employed people launch a business based on their specific skills to satisfy customers in the marketplace. Many S quadrant people (like private practice doctors, lawyers, accountants) get paid per service or task. This typically allows them to make more money and have more control over their futures than employees have. Control is important to S quadrant inhabitants, as most of them started a company because they felt more secure controlling their own destiny than relying upon others.

Indeed, that is precisely why I left AC Rochester and started my own engineering consulting company. I leveraged the recognition I had received from winning a National Technical Benchmarking Award and the skills I learned through technical benchmarking at AC Rochester to move from the E quadrant to the S quadrant. I felt more secure in my own ability to perform and believed I could build an S-business around teaching the benchmarking process to other companies. The next thing I knew, I was traveling around the country building my own self- employed business model, making more money per hour than I ever had before.

Unfortunately, while there are many upsides in the S quadrant, there are also some downsides. For one thing, I discovered that building a big consulting company meant the willingness to travel around the globe. However, with four young children at home at the time, I wasn't excited to do this. After all, what's the point of having children if I rarely see them? For another, I realized that in order to make money, I still had to sell my time. I had, in reality, merely traded a dollars-per-hour job for a dollars-per-service self-employed business. Regardless of how ambitious I was, I was still caught in the money-for-time trap. I finally understood why Kiyosaki emphasized, "Never invest in a business where the system goes home at night," because I was the system that went home at night! In other words, the business could only get as big as the amount of hours I was willing to invest, and this limited the success of my (and every other) S-business owner.

Finally, I found that in the S quadrant, I went from having one boss (as an employee) to having numerous bosses (customers) with conflicting agendas. In effect, it became increasingly difficult to satisfy all my customers, and I knew it would only get worse the bigger my business grew. In a sense, moving from the E quadrant to the S quadrant was like jumping from the frying pan into the fire. True, I made more money, but I also increased my time, travel, and responsibilities with no end in sight. S-business owners are like barge operators who make money by carrying cars across a river. While they can make good money, they are limited by how many times they are willing and able to drive the barge from one side to the other. Curiously, even though I told everyone I owned my own business, I soon realized the business actually owned me.

Business Owner Quadrant: "Per Relationship" Pros and Cons

My personal breakthrough occurred when I began studying B-business owners and discovered they made money based upon a system satisfying the customer's needs. If an S-business owner is like a barge owner, then a B-business owner is someone who builds a bridge instead. With a bridge, the cars can transport themselves across the river by paying a toll to use the business system created by the B-business owner.

The benefits of building a B-business were easy to identify: the business works even when you are not there, and with routine bridge maintenance, the tolls create a daily income stream not directly tied to how many hours or how many tasks the owner performs. In essence, the business system works day and night to satisfy customers. Long term, this sounds much more enjoyable than working twelve to sixteen hours per day the rest of my life.

I remember hearing Michael Dell (a gentleman just a couple of years older than me) give a talk to the Detroit Economic Club when he was worth around $21.5 billion. Needless to say, my net worth at the time was slightly under $21.5 billion (maybe $21.499 billion short or so!). I couldn't understand how Dell could achieve more than all the salaries of all the engineers I worked with when I knew he could not be working nearly as many hours as all my engineer friends. Even if Dell were five times smarter and worked twice as hard (he couldn't work any harder since I routinely put in twelve-hour days), then he should have been around ten times wealthier than I was, not millions of times wealthier! This helped me see the difference between the E and S quadrants (which trade time for money) and the B quadrant (which builds leaders and systems to satisfy customers). The former are limited by the amount of hours in a day, while the latter is limited only by the amount of customers who choose to use the systematic solution to satisfy their needs.

I finally understood why the key to escaping the Financial Matrix is to build a system that results in a business asset. Since the system asset is what satisfies the customer and makes money rather than a person, the asset can work indefinitely without getting tired or needing sleep. As a result, the bigger the business gets, the more it frees a person financially from the time/money trap. Now I knew I would be stuck in the Financial Matrix for decades unless I learned to build a B-business by leading people and building systems just as had Sam Walton and the other successful B quadrant business owners did.

The systems side wasn't going to be a problem since I was a manufacturing systems engineer. However, the people side, for this headstrong engineer, was not going to be easy, because I tested extremely high in process skills and low in people skills in every personality test. In fact, my high school yearbook stated under my senior picture, "Arguing, arguing, early and late, if a line were crooked, he'd argue it straight!" To this day, I have no idea who inserted that in our yearbook.

Still, when the dream is big enough, a person can change the facts, and I needed to learn people skills. With time, I learned that assembling a leadership team and helping them achieve their goals and dreams was even more fun than creating a workable system, but this took time. Indeed, the thought of working with people, at first, produced only fear and trepidation. Nonetheless if the path to freedom required we develop people and systems to create a business asset for ongoing income, then that exactly what Laurie and I would do.

The concept is nothing new, for an ancient Chinese proverb states, "If you want one year of prosperity, grow grain. If you want ten years of prosperity, grow trees. If you want 100 years of prosperity, grow people." I wasn't exactly sure how to do this, but committed to do whatever it would take (legally, morally, and ethically) to learn how to build people the way I knew how to build systems.

Naturally, the downside of a B-business is that it requires time and effort to develop the leadership and systems mindset. Further, unlike a job where a person gets paid while on the clock, a B-business owner only gets paid when his business system satisfies the customer. This can take years to perfect, and some people do not have the perseverance to stick it out. Perhaps this is why so few build a B-business since it takes more time than today's microwave age is willing to give to get results. There are simply no guarantees in a B-business unless one is willing to invest the time to create a workable system. Some would see this as not worth the risk, but I viewed it as my only pathway to escape the Financial Matrix.

Moreover, while the work is tough for a period, the results are enjoyed for life. One of my early mentors taught me, "When the going gets tough, the tough get going." I used this saying many times in my life to get going when things were tough. Eventually, I developed another saying: "You either hate losing enough to change, or you hate changing enough to lose." I didn't necessarily like change, but I *hated* losing, and I knew I had to make the leap from the E and S quadrants to the B quadrant (and then to the I quadrant). To do so, I would need new information because the thinking that had produced my existing results was learned from E and S mentors. I knew that to make new decisions, I would need new information, so I started a daily regimen of reading personal development books and listening to audios to make myself into the leader capable of succeeding in a B quadrant business.

Investor Quadrant: "Per ROI" Pros and Cons

The I quadrant consists of investors who are free from the Financial Matrix through applying consistent defense and offense to their finances. The financially free investors have wiped out all their debts (including home mortgages) and have built investments producing enough income to enable them to live indefinitely outside of the Financial Matrix. In other words, they are debt-free and cash-rich, and they receive enough ongoing income to live financially free by purchasing bridges built by others. This should be the long-term goal of every person in the civilized world: to enjoy significant ongoing incomes without significant ongoing time investments.

The I quadrant investors have applied long-term dreams and practiced short-term denials and now enjoy the power of long-term duplication in their favor. Indeed, when debt-free B or I quadrant people go to bed at night, they wake up wealthier—a sure sign that they have broken free from the Financial Matrix. Investors now have money making money for them. And when their I quadrant income is enough to support their lifestyle, they can live indefinitely without income from the E, S, and even the B quadrants. Whereas every other quadrant invests time to make money (even the B quadrant invests time to build people and systems), the I quadrant is the only one that invests money to make money and thus buys back time.

Naturally, the I quadrant upside is the money, time, and freedom from the Financial Matrix, while the downside is simply the time and effort invested to reach it (unless the person inherited wealth). I believe, since it takes effort to live no matter which quadrant one chooses to start in, we may as well apply the effort to build a B-business to free us from the time-for-dollars trap. Once this effort is successful, the I quadrant beckons (see Chris Bray's and my book, Beyond Financial Fitness, for more details), where money makes the person more money, and freedom to live his dreams is the reward. Indeed, an employee, a self-employed person, and a B-business owner can all reach the I quadrant and escape the Financial Matrix, but the fastest route is to leverage the left-side quadrants for short-term security while building the right-side quadrants for long-term dreams. Let me repeat that: The fastest route for most people to become Financially Free is to leverage the left-side quadrants for short-term security while they focus on creating a B-business (systems making money) that eventually leads to I quadrant (money making money) lifestyle and dream fulfillment.

The long-term dream (escape from the Financial Matrix) that Laurie and I imagined in late 1993 became a reality over the next decade. By 2004, we had paid off our mortgage and have lived as debt-free Financially Free people ever since. Over the last couple of years, our I quadrant investments have returned enough to support our lifestyle. This allows us to build businesses to fulfill our calling rather than pay bills.

The same I quadrant lifestyle is available to anyone willing to apply the principles taught in the Financial Fitness and the Beyond FFPs consistently. I don't promise *easy*, but I do promise *worth it*.

Dan and Lisa Hawkins' Story

Dan and Lisa Hawkins (to use another of the Life founding couples as an illustration) are an excellent example of a young couple who took Warren Buffett's advice to heart. When they studied the principles in the FFP, they realized their lack of capital was hindering their ability to go on offense. To use a football analogy, their defense was so poor that their offense rarely stepped onto the field. Through mentorship, however, Dan and Lisa got serious about debt reduction. Although they only made $50,000 per year combined, they quickly wiped out debt by applying the proper financial principles. For instance, Dan was spending eight to ten dollars every day on vending machine snacks and drinks and an additional five to ten dollars on lunch. These expenses were quickly cut out as Dan began packing a lunch from home and curtailing his soda pop consumption on the job. They also canceled their cable subscription, began to read more, and used the money they normally spent on movies and dinners out for business training and personal development materials instead.

Gaining confidence in practicing short-term denials, Dan sold his hotrod Mustang and paid cash for a $3,000 replacement vehicle. He then used the remaining cash to pay off Lisa's car, effectively eliminating $600 of monthly payments. With the extra monthly cash flow, Dan and Lisa paid off one credit card and then another, and over a couple of years, they eliminated two car loans, several credit card balances, an ATV loan, a computer loan, student loans, and finally their mortgage!

Dan and Lisa disciplined themselves to follow four simple principles, which are among the forty-seven principles taught in the defense, offense, and playing field of the FFP:

1. When you receive income, immediately put 10% toward savings.
2. Then, minimize expenses (self-entertainment) and maximize investments (self-education).
3. Service all debts with minimum payments except the highest interest rate debt, which should be paid down with all extra funds.
4. After the first three items are done, pay the rest of the bills.

Once the process was rolling, the victories being achieved created momentum for future successful outcomes. Not surprisingly, thanks to their disciplined approach to finances, the Hawkins family eventually accumulated thousands of dollars in savings. With their business income continuing to grow and all debt eliminated, their nest egg grew rapidly. This allowed them the freedom to purchase a house three times as big as their previous one with a substantial down payment. As Dan and Lisa built up their savings, they retired debt and used the larger cash flow to increase investment in themselves and their growing business. Newer cars and better vacations followed as the Hawkins family lived a cash lifestyle in which they only spent money they had already earned. Still, they kept saving a portion of all income. Amazingly, through increases in their business and consistent financial discipline, the Hawkins family went on to buy an 8,500-square-foot custom home on over twenty acres, paying almost 50% equity at closing (goal is to pay off mortgage within five years). Dreams do come true for those who read, listen to, learn, and apply the timeless principles of financial fitness.

Today, Dan and Lisa lead a multimillion-dollar leadership company and speak around North America teaching financial and leadership principles to others. By following Buffett's two key wealth-building principles of getting out of debt and investing in themselves, Dan and Lisa Hawkins went from living in dread to living their dreams.

The man who never has money enough to pay his debts has too much of something else.

—JAMES LENDALL BASFORD

CHAPTER 8

LONG-TERM DUPLICATION

Now that we have implemented long-term dreams for the future (to break free from the Financial Matrix) and are using these long-term dreams to practice short-term denials (playing defense), we are ready to go on offense by utilizing long-term duplication.

Before we get into the details of offense, let me ask you a question. If I owned Microsoft and offered to sell it to you for $100, would you buy it? How about Exxon Mobil Corporation for $100? Finally, if I offered you Chipotle Mexican Grill for $100, would you be in? If you are anything like me, you would enthusiastically agree to all three bargains, even if you don't have any expertise or experience in the three businesses. Why? Because you, just like me, don't care what business it is so long as it works (and is legal, moral, and ethical).[4]

Business author Michael Gerber taught similarly when he explained that the key to a turnkey business system has "less to do with what's done in a business and more to do with how it's done. The commodity isn't what's important—the way it's delivered is." In a similar fashion, Life has created a turnkey marketing system for people to plug into and apply, and with time, the combination of defense and offense helps them escape the Financial Matrix by building a business asset.

To be sure, in order to build a business asset and obtain financial freedom, one must move from the left side of the CASHFLOW Quadrant to the right side. However, quitting one's job or S-business is risky and not feasible when starting for most people. Thus, the best plan to escape the Financial Matrix usually includes working on the left side of the Quadrant to pay bills and building the right-side B-business through creating leaders and a turnkey system for future dreams. This plan provides the security of a steady income on the left side, which provides time to develop the appropriate skills to create a B-business system. Entrepreneurial risk, that is to say, is greatly reduced by leveraging the security of the left-side quadrants while striving for the financial independence offered on the right side.

In particular, Laurie and I were looking for a business that leveraged the latest technologies and strategies to give ourselves the best opportunity to succeed in our own B-Business. When the cofounders created Life, we did so by tying into four important world trends:

- Home-Based Businesses
- The Internet
- Word-of-Mouth Marketing
- Franchising

Home-Based Business (HBB)

A home-based business (HBB) was a necessity since Laurie and I didn't have the financial wherewithal to invest in a bricks-and-mortar company. Indeed, the cost of rent, inventory, and employees takes most of a start-up's revenue and leaves it on the edge of fiscal solvency. We knew our financial situation was tenuous enough without the additional expenses associated with a traditional business. The goal was to get out of debt, not go further into it, and only an HBB model provided us with the opportunity to win or lose based upon our efforts.

Moreover, there are legal tax deductions available to people who are building a home business that are not accessible to employees. An HBB, in other words, permits the owner to write off legitimate business expenses while keeping overall expenses low by using the home and other assets he or she regularly utilizes anyway. This trend has leveled the entrepreneurial playing field and allows people to compete with hunger rather than with capital. Laurie and I may have lacked capital, but we made up for it with our hunger and the benefits of building our business from home. I worked at a job during the day to pay our bills, Laurie stayed at home to raise our family, and we both worked our HBB at night to achieve our dreams.

The Internet

There has never been a better time to start a home-based business because the Internet has changed the rules of the game. Indeed, the "bricks-versus-clicks" revolution has made it possible for people to build a business from their home that generates more revenue than the largest Wal-Mart store. Furthermore, by leveraging the Internet, an HBB can do this for a fraction of the cost of a traditional retail store. The Internet allows people to offer products around the world from their home without having to have inventory tied up in each state, province, or country. This is a huge competitive advantage for small entrepreneurs over large corporations. Interestingly, although most people understand the Internet has changed the rules of the game and have even purchased some products online themselves, few have learned how to create a profitable online business. Consequently, when people combine the benefits of an Internet model and an HBB, they have the benefits of left-side quadrant security with right-side quadrant opportunity (low cost, low risk, and high profit potential). This is the safest formula to follow for people who want to make the entrepreneurial leap to escape the Financial Matrix.

Word-of-Mouth Marketing

Life leverages word-of-mouth marketing to compound its growth. Instead of paying millions of dollars per year to advertise in print, radio, or TV, Life instead rewards people who recommend our products. This is a major competitive advantage! For example, authors Huba and McConnell proclaimed, "Word-of-mouth is THE valuable currency in today's advertising-saturated world." Meanwhile, Nielsen Global Trust in Advertising noted that 92% of respondents surveyed trusted recommendations received from friends about products and services. Last but not least, a recent McKinsey study identified word-of-mouth as the most effective form of marketing and advertising in the world. According to the McKinsey study, word-of-mouth marketing generates twice as much sales as paid advertising, and over 50% of all purchases are influenced by word-of-mouth. Indeed, the buzz generated by word-of-mouth marketing is vital to the growth of a company.

Because word-of-mouth marketing is so effective, Life built its entire marketing and advertising budget around it. We reward loyal customers and members who are effective in recommending our products to others.

All word-of-mouth marketing can be boiled down to a three-step process:

1. Discovery: Somebody encounters a new idea.
2. Wow: This person is convinced that the idea is worth sharing.
3. The Share: The person shares the new information with others.

Once this process loop is started, the share stage for one person corresponds with the discovery stage of another one, and the word-of-mouth chain reaction has started. Seth Godin, author of *Unleashing the Ideavirus*, emphasized the importance of making it easy to share the product or company's message: "How easy is it for an end user to spread this particular ideavirus? Can I click one button or mention some magic phrase, or do I have to go through hoops and risk embarrassment to tell someone about it?"

Franchising Model

Finally, the most successful businesses in the world follow a business format franchise model. Companies like McDonald's, Starbucks, and Jiffy Lube, to name just a few, have each built a predictable process to satisfy customers' needs. Few people have built a successful business; therefore, the turnkey system, designed by those who have the experience and results, is leveraged to allow average people to produce un-average results. Michael Gerber explained how Ray Kroc, the pioneering genius of the turnkey business system, developed the original McDonald's system:

Given the failure rate of most small businesses, he must have realized a crucial fact: for McDonald's to be a predictable success, the business would have to work, because the franchisee, left to his own devices, most assuredly wouldn't! Once he understood this, Ray Kroc's problem became his opportunity. Forced to create a business that worked in order to sell it, he also created a business that would work once it was sold, no matter who bought it. Armed with that realization, he set about the task of creating a foolproof, predictable business. A systems-dependent business, not a people-dependent business. A business that would work without him.

In the same way, Life set out to create a turnkey marketing system that would work for anyone who did the work of leveraging it. In other words, the entrepreneur does not have to be smart enough or work and invest in order to create the system, but he or she does have to be smart enough and work to leverage it. Life focuses on fulfilling Warren Buffett's two key points for financial success (you'll remember this by now!), eliminating debt at all costs (defense) and investing in self-education (offense). By tapping into Life's number one selling product, the FFP, people will learn the principles of financial defense, offense, and the playing field (the Financial Matrix). Furthermore, Life has created a turnkey business operation that allows people to work on the left side of the CASHFLOW Quadrant to eliminate debt and then invest some of the savings to build a right-side quadrant B-Business. At the same time, people will develop themselves and others by leveraging the turnkey Life Training Marketing System.

Life is the best of both worlds because it teaches people to leverage the defense and security of the left side and the offense and freedom of the right side to produce the desired results. With time and effort, people can generate enough money in their B-business to exit the left side entirely and enjoy their business asset while building I quadrant investment income. This is the path to freedom from the Financial Matrix.

The 3 Cs for Successful Internet Companies

When I heard Michael Dell speak at the Detroit Economics Club, he stated that any business that didn't get online within the next couple of years would be out of business. He used a model he called "Direct from Dell," a catalogue ordering system that cut out middlemen even before the Internet was commercially available. As a result, he was one of the earliest online adopters. Later in his talk, he listed the "3 Cs" necessary to succeed online:

- Content
- Commerce
- Community

Chris Brady and I were there to hear this talk in late 1999. Today, we have built our entire business around being world-class in these three areas. While some companies produce great informational products (Dave Ramsey, Tony Robbins, etc.) and others have innovative methods of commerce (Amazon, Alibaba, etc.) and still others have loyal communities (Apple, Harley-Davidson, etc.), only Life is building a business intersecting all 3 Cs.

First, Life begins with world-class informational content to help people escape the Financial Matrix that is second to none in the marketplace. Second, we married the products to a world-class commerce section with the best word-of-mouth marketing compensation (see the Life Compensation Plan Brochure for details). Finally, Life has assembled a leadership team with tens of thousands (Life conventions routinely fill stadiums across North America) of enthusiastic, knowledgeable, and loyal members who represent the true product of our business, namely, changed lives. In a dark world, Life's mission is to shine light into the darkness to help people see a way to escape from the bondage of debt.

Being world-class in any one of the 3 Cs is impressive, but creating a business that is the intersection of world-class performance in each of the 3 Cs has really been done until now. Over the next decade, Life will become a household name in the financial, personal, and professional development fields as it helps millions of people across the globe live debt-free and thousands more be job-optional through building a B-business bridge to escape the Financial Matrix. Not surprisingly, Life realized that few people are like the young Solomon, who prayed for wisdom and had all other things added unto him; instead, most are more pragmatic and seek answers to their financial challenges first. Of course, once Life proves the FFP is effective in eliminating the debt that has trapped them, many of the people who experienced the change in finances go on to seek long-term wisdom as well. People, as a result, are not just getting financially free, but are also gaining wisdom that sets them free in other areas of life.

Content

The content side of an Internet business is the website and the products available. As I've stated before, Life's top product category is the Financial Fitness suite of products and services. This program teaches people how to play successful *defense* and live below their means while also giving them the guidelines and options of how to launch a financial *offense*. Moreover and uniquely, it teaches customers about the Financial Matrix and the *playing field* they find themselves on. The beautiful thing about the Financial Fitness suite of products is that it not only provides the information to help customers get out of debt, stay out of debt, and to then prosper financially, but it also offers the tools required do so. These include a free website for organizing one's financial goals, a Financial Fitness Services subscription that provides aggregated coupons for saving money on everyday purchases, a mobile expense tracker to help customers accurately track where their money goes, credit monitoring and identity theft protection and insurance, computer virus protection, and prepaid legal services including preparation of a free will and testament.

Finally, though, since Buffett said to invest in self-education, Life provides an entire array of life-changing information for personal and professional development as well. But because finances seem to be the area in which the majority of people need the most urgent help, Life usually concentrates on the financial area first in order to help people get some financial breathing room.

Commerce

The commerce piece of an Internet business is how products are produced directly by the manufacturer and delivered directly to the customer without costly marketing and advertising. This generates an impressive level of savings because Life ships or downwards its award-winning financial and leadership materials directly to customers and members who are the word-of-mouth marketers. Low inventory and overhead costs along with high-value proposition products separate Life from the rest of the financial and leadership fields. Life, as a result, flows the money saved in the commerce steps to compensate its members who share the life-changing information with others.

Consider this common scenario: Families realize they are in debt and need to get out of the Financial Matrix, so they purchase the FFP to learn how to play defense. However, once they start wiping out debt, they realize it may take twenty to thirty years to escape the Financial Matrix entirely. Some are okay with this and continue moving ahead, dreaming of a debt-free retirement. Others, in contrast, may choose to speed up the process by going on offense. They begin building a bridge (business asset) from their current reality toward their future dreams by becoming a member of Life. At this point, they leverage the experiences and results of other successful bridge builders to build their own business asset. In the process, they shorten the twenty- to-thirty-year plan for freedom into a possible to- to five-year plan. Finished bridges allow families to enjoy quality time because they are no longer barge-working their whole life. A bridge is different from a barge because even though it took time, effort, and skills to build, the bridge continues to produce results even when the bridge builder isn't there. Building bridges through which products and services flow to customers and bonuses flow to members is how the Life community utilizes the power of long-term duplication.

With few exceptions, practically everyone needs what Life offers: improved financial management (defense, which reduces expenses), wealth thinking (investments in self and business assets), and an understanding of the playing field (the Financial Matrix). By learning how to play defense and then also going on offense, people can live the life they've always wanted by losing the debt they've never needed.

Community

The community section, however, is by far the most important because in Life, people are in business for themselves but not by themselves. Each person or couple has a support team to teach them how to apply the defense, offense, and playing field of finances to achieve their dreams.

Dell said back in 1999 that he had not at that time entirely discovered how to create a loyal community, but Life has through compensating its members for recommending its products. Life has created a *Compensated Community* that pays members a bonus based upon sales volume moved per month. The more sales volume produced, the more income generated.

If a person recommends the FFP or other products to just a few customers or members, he or she will receive a smaller bonus, but if that person recommends products to many customers, he or she can be rewarded for the results produced. Life and the members work together, and no commission is paid until the products are moved to customers. This is why word-of-mouth Compensated Communities are so efficient and effective in marketing products and services.

It's important to note that regardless of when or where a person starts in the community, he or she can achieve a higher compensation than the person who introduced him or her to Life. Since compensation is based on sales volume through the communities each person builds, anyone can make the most money based on his or her leadership and results. Unlike a typical job, where the boss always makes more than those who report to him or her, the performer gets paid the most regardless of where he or she starts in the organization.

Imagine as the community grows, a person begins making part-time what he or she makes at his or her full-time job. Once this happens, the person can quickly wipe out debt by living on his or her job income and paying down debt from his or her newly created bridge-building business asset. Of course, when someone starts eliminating debt and building an asset, that person becomes very loyal to his or her own products, since he or she sees the results of the new knowledge being applied to his or her personal and professional life.

Finally, Life's turnkey business system includes a *Team Approach* to building the first team ("apprenticeship team") together. The best way for a person to learn how to build a community (bridge) is to have one of the leaders model and message the proper principles and practices. Team Approach is a systematic method for modeling and messaging so the amateur apprentice can quickly become a Power Player by learning from someone who has already done it. Building an apprenticeship community isn't just about those you know who might be interested in better financial defense and offense; rather, it's about those a team of people know. This means that, working together with a team, you can create much greater results than you would be able to accomplish alone. John D. Rockefeller taught a similar concept when he said, "I would rather earn 1% off 100 people's efforts than 100% of my own efforts."

Claude and Lana Hamilton's Story

Claude and Lana Hamilton met and married while serving in the Canadian Armed Forces. It wasn't long before the Hamiltons realized that the forced separations and low pay were not a good foundation for building a family. Moreover, they struggled to meet their bills and accumulated tens of thousands of dollars of debt in the Financial Matrix. Fortunately, the Hamiltons refused to stay there. Through applying the principles taught in the FFP, they disciplined themselves to live below their means and invest the difference in their own business asset. Because they drove used cars and lived in a rented house, many of their friends thought they were crazy. The climb out of debt took several years, but the key was the Hamiltons knew it was their only shot. Instead of focusing on their excuses, they focused on their reasons why. They used the financial and time challenges as fuel to drive them forward in building a business asset. Today, the Hamiltons are living their dreams, having built large Compensated Communities across the United States and Canada as well as having built one of the largest houses in Halifax. Claude sits on the Policy Council Board as one of the founders of Life, and the

Hamiltons are leading many others toward freedom from the Financial Matrix.

Summary

In closing, just as the Northern states created an Underground Railroad to help Physical Matrix slaves escape north to Canada and freedom, Life has become an "Underground Railroad" to help Financial Matrix subjects escape to financial freedom. We created the FFP to teach the defense, offense, and playing field of finances. Further, we created a turnkey business asset for people who choose to share the FFP strategies with others. When they build a Compensated Community and leverage the proven Life Training Marketing System, they are building a B quadrant business by developing people and leveraging systems.

Now it's up to you.

Just like Neo in the movie *The Matrix*, you have to choose between the red pill and the blue pill set before you. Are you ready to unplug from the Financial Matrix?

In the movie, Neo asks Morpheus why more people aren't searching for the answers about the nature of the Matrix. The answer Morpheus gives Neo (with my additions in brackets) applies similarly to the Financial Matrix today:

> The [Financial] Matrix is a system, Neo. That system is our enemy. But when you're inside, you look around. What do you see? Business people, teachers, lawyers, carpenters—the very minds of the people we are trying to save. But until we do, these people are still a part of that system, and that makes them our enemy. You have to understand, most of these people are not ready to be unplugged. And many of them are

so inert, so hopelessly dependent on the [debt] system that they will fight to protect it.[5]

As we wrap up our time together, I want to express how proud I am of you for finishing this book. So few people ever read a book cover to cover. Now the ball is in your court. I have presented the truth about what the Financial Matrix, how it captures people through debt, and how a person can escape the Financial Matrix system of control. Will you join the Underground Railroad and free yourself from the Financial Matrix, or will you fight to protect the web of debt that has enslaved you?

Perhaps, like my conversation with Laurie years ago, today is one of the turning points in your life. All true change begins with a new decision that leads to new actions. I pray you decide wisely.

FREQUENTLY
ASKED QUESTIONS

1. Are there legal tax deductions available for people who build a home-based business?

For people building a true business, there are legal tax deductions for things such as training expenses, meeting expenses, and business-building car mileage. Consult with a business accountant to ensure you are tracking and recording all business expenses properly.

2. What is the difference between a Compensated Community and a pyramid?

I am often asked if network marketing is a pyramid scheme. My reply is that corporations really are pyramid schemes. A corporation has only one person at the top, generally the CEO, and everyone else below.

—DONALD TRUMP, AMERICAN BUSINESS MAGNATE,
AND PRESIDENT OF THE UNITED STATES

Every reputable direct sales organization separates itself from pyramid schemes and scams by ensuring significant sales of its products to customers, proper representations of the incomes possible through the sales of those products, and the absence of pay for recruiting. At Life, we are very committed to being a model direct sales organization upholding the highest ideals of the profession. As such, at Life, there are no required purchases on the part of members whatsoever. All bonuses and sales commissions are paid *only* if the member meets a minimum monthly customer sales requirement of $100 ($400 if the sales are made of our Financial Fitness Bullion Reserve products). There are no "auto ship" programs that members must be on in order to receive bonuses, and there are no "fast start" bonuses or anything of the sort that pay for recruiting new Life members. Also, we have a comprehensive Income Disclosure Statement that shares the details of the performance of Life members that every prospective Life member must review before enrolling. We are also very proud of the many ways in which Life members profit from the sale of our products, as listed below:

1. Retail Sales Margin:
   - Life Members earn a 15% commission on the PV of all products sold to Registered Customers.

2. The "3 for FREE" Customer Referral Programs:
   - Is a Customer Referral Program for both Members and Registered Customers that helps encourage customers to refer other customers to our product subscriptions.

3. Customer Pool Bonus (CPB):
   - Is a bonus paid quarterly based on a Life member's total quarterly sales to Registered Customers.

4. Cumulative Customer Bonus:
   - Is a bonus paid annually based on a Life member's total annual sales to Registered Customers.

5. Customer Bonus:
   - In addition to the 15% commission, Members earn a monthly commission based on their monthly customer sales.

Further, to provide additional incentives and a little healthy competition, Life rewards Members through two sales contests – one being a quarterly Customers Sales Contest that focuses solely on the retail sales of a pre-determined featured product, and the other being a Top Retail Sales Team Contest. The Customer Sales Contest provides cash and travel rewards above and beyond all of those listed above, and both contests provide recognition at Life's quarterly National Conventions.

3. What was the legal dispute between some of the Life leaders, Quixtar, and MonaVie about?

I get asked this question periodically even though the dispute ended way back in 2010. Still, I believe the highlights from the issue can help people understand the principles Life is founded upon. Before discussing the details, however, I think it's important to share that I have no hard feelings for anyone who worked with Quixtar or currently works with Amway. As a matter of fact, I still have friends that work within the company. I believe life is too short to carry grudges and what is past is past. Further, I have heard from several sources that Amway has softened its litigation policy against leaders who want to leave the company. For this, I am thankful. Finally, I learned a ton during my time with Quixtar and had many memorable experiences. As a result, I have taken the good, flushed the bad, and moved ahead with no animosity.

Before Life was launched, Laurie and I, along with some of the other top leaders, worked with the Quixtar company to build our community (business asset). Quixtar was a North American Internet-based direct sales business started by the owners of Amway but set up as a separate company from its parent. This was an important feature to me because I had joined Amway in 1993 when I learned they were developing an interactive distribution model to combine high-tech and high-touch. Regretfully, however, by 1998, I realized this was more hype than substance and had not come to fruition. Since Laurie and I had no interest in building a traditional Amway business, we planned on starting a new venture.

Nevertheless, after hearing Ken McDonald (Quixtar's first managing director) share his long-term dream for an online model that would be a separate company backed by Amway money, we were intrigued. Accordingly, in 1999, we did not renew our Amway distributorship and joined Quixtar instead as an Independent Business Owner (IBO). The online model fit our young and hungry team perfectly. In fact, from 1999 through 2007, Laurie and I led the fastest growing organization within the company. We grew from several hundred to over ten thousand people attending events, and our sales increased from a couple hundred thousand dollars to over one hundred million dollars! In addition, many other teams sought our training and started growing also, resulting in nearly another hundred million dollars in volume. Our training organization, in other words, was responsible for nearly two hundred million dollars of Quixtar's total sales.

Unfortunately, the rest of Quixtar was not doing well, mainly because the older, more mature organizations seemed unable to adjust to building an online business. I saw the loss of confidence and numbers firsthand because I was asked to speak consistently to Quixtar groups across North America. Dismally, instead of growing into the hundred-billion-dollar company Ken McDonald and other top leaders envisioned, Quixtar leveled off around a billion dollars (even with our team's meteoric growth). In fact, many of the top leaders lost half their numbers or more as they struggled to marry high-touch communities with the high-tech online environment. Nonetheless, I didn't realize the precarious nature of the Quixtar business until Ken McDonald abruptly announced his retirement in 2005, despite having flown to see me just weeks earlier to discuss future strategies. To say I was disappointed would be an understatement (Ken and I worked well together), but I also respected Quixtar's right to choose its leadership team.

Curiously, however, Quixtar's new managing director was also an Amway vice-president. Although I thought this was strange, I was assured on numerous occasions that the two were still separate corporations and the change in management was merely to help Quixtar increase its sales. As a result, the 2007 announcement that Quixtar was closing its doors and that all its Independent Business Owners (IBOs) would be transitioned into Amway shocked me. This was unacceptable for several reasons. For one thing, I was not in Amway (having purposefully not renewed when Quixtar launched), nor did I want to be in Amway. For another, I had told tens of thousands of people that they were Independent Business Owners affiliated with Quixtar just as the IBO moniker implied. True, Quixtar was owned by the founders of Amway, but they were allegedly separate companies with separate field organizations. Indeed, I must have repeated this message of separate companies a thousand times because that is what Ken McDonald and the rest of Quixtar's management team had told all of us. In sum, the deal had been changed, or

I had been misled and thus found myself in the inadvertent position of being asked to likewise do so to others.

For me, the whole conflict was a moral issue. On one hand, I knew Quixtar (like any company) had the power to break its commitments to its customers, but it didn't have the power to avoid the subsequent fallout. On the other hand, how could I represent a company to others that I believed had misrepresented itself to me? Indeed, leadership is character in motion, and without trust, it's impossible for any leader to get in motion. Nevertheless, quitting my independent business was not as simple as it sounded since Amway had stated its intention to litigate against any leader attempting to leave Amway/Quixtar (indeed, hundreds were sued before and after me). Not surprisingly, the legal risk intimidated many other leaders into submission, but it only emboldened our leadership team. If we stayed with Amway because we feared litigation, then we would be imprisoned into Amway's Legal Matrix and not truly independent anyway. How could we ever recommend others to join us as Independent Business Owners when we knew in our hearts that the term was no longer true? Although the easiest thing to do would have been to rejoin Amway, announce my retirement, and slowly watch my groups dissolve, this was morally unconscionable. I also doubted Amway's antiquated business model could work in the Internet-savvy North American market regardless of how many millions Amway spent on television advertisements. (Amway no longer discloses North American sales volume, but it is rumored to have dropped precipitously.) How could Laurie and I in good conscience give up our purpose and principles for profit while our community suffered? And yet, I also knew that I would be sued by Amway (a multibillion- dollar international company) if I didn't agree to its plan. Financially, this was a lose-lose scenario. Neither option, in other words, was without massive risk and challenges, but leaders are paid to make decisions, and it was time to make a decision.

Thankfully, I had great leaders like Chris Brady, Claude Hamilton, George Guzzardo, and Bill Lewis (interestingly, I barely knew my good friend and Life cofounder Dan Hawkins at the time), who all believed we should choose character over convenience. Accordingly, I called a meeting with Quixtar's top management to announce my immediate resignation and intention to sit out Quixtar's six-month noncompete period. My plan was to form a new company and build our businesses entirely separate from either Quixtar or Amway. Disastrously, however, instead of accepting my resignation, Amway announced it was "firing" me (how a company can fire an Independent Business Owner is still inexplicable to me) and proceeded to call each of the leaders in our community to demand they choose either Quixtar (soon to be Amway) or staying with me. Of course, the field leaders had no idea what Quixtar was talking about since I had not announced to anyone (except a handful of my top leaders) any plans to start another business.

Amway's management team had no idea the hornets' nest they had knocked over. People in our organization were already upset at the name change, and now Amway/Quixtar compounded its errors by "firing" Chris Brady and me, manufacturing press releases, and issuing ultimatums. Not surprisingly, Quixtar paid for its hubris. In our organization alone, over 50,000 IBOs chose to resign rather than switch to Amway. Of course, Amway (true to its promise) initiated multimillion-dollar court and arbitration proceedings against me and others. The financial stakes were high since we had already lost our business incomes and now risked bankruptcy. Evidently, the plan appeared to be to sue people into submission.

Consequently, starting our own company was out of the question. It would be foolhardy to attempt when a multibillion-dollar company was seeking to squash us. I didn't feel that falling on my own sword and hurting the many people who followed me out of Quixtar was the proper plan. Rather, I needed a plan for survival until Amway realized we would not surrender our principles no matter what the consequences. Accordingly, I sought to join another company so I could earn money to help support our growing legal mess (tens of millions of dollars). Of course, I ensured, upfront, that once the legal battles were over, we would be free to start our own business if we still desired to.

Fortunately, I found Dallin Larsen, the 2009 Ernst & Young Entrepreneur of the Year and founder of MonaVie. MonaVie, in 2008, was one of the fastest growing companies in direct sales (Dallin retired in 2014 and MonaVie was subsequently sold to Jeunesse in 2015). While he benefited from bringing in our large organization (millions of dollars per month in volume), he also had taken a huge risk. In truth, I do not see how we would have survived without working with MonaVie. As expected, Amway subsequently sued MonaVie (I commend the company's persistence) and countless more millions were spent battling the behemoth. Fortunately, Dallin Larsen did not flinch and followed through on everything he committed to despite several years of resulting legal harassment.

Finally, in 2010, a global settlement was reached. After much pain and pressure (the battle had left no one unscathed), the war was over. I believe Amway finally realized the IBOs who resigned were not coming back, and we had enough funding to continue the legal battles indefinitely. As a result, the biggest leadership challenge we had ever faced was finally over. Our community was *free!* This was our team's finest moment.

I have never been more proud of any group of leaders for they had survived over three years (2007 through 2010) without surrendering, some even choosing to declare bankruptcy rather than give in to Amway's legal demands.

In closing, many times during the struggle, I had told the leaders that those who stayed would be champions. It is inspiring to see how many achievers stayed with us to finish the million-person mission. These men and women are the ones who dreamed, the ones who dared, and the ones who sacrificed to make Life a reality. Although I have read thousands of books on businesses, I have never found a more inspiring example of a group of common people willing to face uncommon giants. Perhaps the best description of the Life pioneers is displayed on a plaque at the Overpass Museum in Carney, Nebraska: "The cowards never started. The weak died on the way. Only the strong survived." If a person is ready to face his or her personal Goliaths, I know of no stronger community to help him or her do so than Life.

4. How is Life different from traditional direct sales companies?

This is a great question and deserves to be answered in several parts.

The majority of Life shares are owned by field leaders. As Chairman of the Board, I make nearly all my income from building my business in the field just like you. As such, I would be crazy to do anything to harm the field leaders because I am one of them. In addition, the other founders (outside of CEO Chris Brady and President Rob Hallstrand, who both started building communities before moving to corporate) build the business just like everyone else and thus earn nearly all their incomes by building communities of customers and members. As a result, the Founders will not tolerate win-lose corporate maneuvers that hurt the field leadership. Furthermore, the Life Coaches have formed a Policy Council that helps create and implement corporate policy and since the Policy Council controls the majority of the shares of Life, the field is protected better than any other company in the profession.

In addition, Life has structured its business to return a minimum of 75% and a maximum of 90% (in 2014 and 2015 combined Life paid out 90%) of all PV to the field leaders. Whereas the rest of the direct sales compensation plans boast between 33% and 55% in PV paid out, Life trumps the field. We do this by focusing upon the information and services sector, a sector known for its low cost and high-value proposition products. We created the compensation structure to ensure the corporate office is fiscally conservative by paying bonuses based upon its cost per dollar of revenue. In a word, all boats rise together when the tide does. The reward systems were designed this way specifically because we learned firsthand what happens when corporate and field leadership have different agendas.

In essence, Life trademarked "Compensated Communities" in order to highlight its four main innovations compared to traditional direct sales:

INNOVATION #1: Higher compensation rates than any competitor we know of, which means that anyone can have success commensurate with the work effort extended over time. The choice is up to each member.

INNOVATION #2: We use a Team Approach to help everyone succeed in business at a whole new level. Leaders help new members market and merchandise to build the "apprenticeship team." In other words, people are in business for themselves, but not by themselves.

INNOVATION #3: Pay raises are based on performance, pure and simple. Members are paid on building communities in which products and services are merchandised. This is significant because it ensures performance, rather than politics, is rewarded. You get to decide if you get a raise, a promotion, and other benefits. (Please see the Life Compensation Plan and Income Disclosure Statement.)

INNOVATION #4: Life provides each member with the exact same compensation deal. *No one* gets a special deal that is not earned through actual performance in numbers and volume. The Life Compensation plan, the Scholarship Program, Year-End Bonuses, even the Fun-n-the-Sun Cruise and volume rebates on training tools are available to all based upon performance, not politics. To use the bridge analogy again, the majority of one's income is made by building bridges, rather than just selling the hammers and nails needed to build them. While hammers, nails, and cement are vital to build a bridge, they are not the business, but only support the main objective, namely, building durable bridges. In a similar fashion, training tools and aids are not the main business and only support the main objective, namely, building long-term sustainable businesses where customers and members are satisfied.

I believe that if the owners of direct sales companies back in the 1960s and 1970s had disciplined themselves to only keep 10% or less of company income and use the other 90% or more to run the company and pay bonuses, direct sales would be as big as discount stores like Wal-Mart and Target today. Instead, most companies take around one-third each for profit, business operations, and field profits. In contrast, Wal-Mart is excited if it hits between only 6% and 10% profit. The discrepancy in profits kept between discount stores and most direct sales companies is, in my opinion, the main reason direct sales has not lived up to its potential growth. A Compensated Community operates best when it ensures the majority of corporate revenues flow to field leaders rather than company executives or owners. As CEO Chris Brady said, "We didn't found this company to make a lot of money; we founded it to pay a lot of money!" This leads me into the final competitive advantage, namely, CEO Chris Brady. Chris is an Inc. magazine Top 40 leader and New York Times bestselling leadership author. We have been business partners and great friends for over twenty years. He is one of the most creative and character-centered people I know. After working with him for an extended period of time, I realized that he refuses to play politics, refuses to pass the buck, and has a burning desire to achieve excellence in everything he does. Indeed, I met him when we were both eighteen-year-old kids about ready to enter engineering school together, and the hunger to excel was present even back then. In fact, he built Life to the Life Coach level before walking away from this income in order to take charge of Life's global business operations as CEO and Creative Director. Chris's friendship and business partnership has been a blessing to our family.

Life's corporate office is located just outside of Raleigh, North Carolina, near where Chris lives. He is responsible for leading the corporate offices, and I am responsible for leading the Compensated Community. Together, along with the rest of the Policy Council, we set the course for Life. Chris and I talk nearly every day to ensure the company and the field leaders are aligned in long-term dreams, culture, and objectives. I believe Life has the right people on the bus, in the right seats on the bus, and now we are driving onward to reach one million people with our life-changing information. We hope you're one of them!

Appendices

The appendix section provides further history and background information on important aspects of this Financial Matrix. While the book is complete without these appendices, I felt many readers would be interested in a deeper look at how the banking system utilizes fractional-reserve banking and the people's lack of understanding of what money is to create the Financial Matrix system of control. With this in mind, the three appendices cover each of these subjects in more detail: 1) What is Fractional-Reserve Banking?, 2) What are the three historical Matrices of Control?, and 3) What is Money? Once the inner-workings of the money system are comprehended, the reader will begin to recognize various aspects of control throughout the market place, leading to an increased motivation to escape the Financial Matrix.

APPENDIX I
What Is Fractional Reserve Banking?

The government-sponsored fractional reserve banking (FRB) system allows banks, in partnership with the central banks, to create the majority of society's money (debt money) out of thin air. Unbelievably, the FRB system permits the banks to create fiat debt money out of thin air but forces borrowers to pay it back through the sweat equity of real production. It's as if the banks have been given a license to make fool's gold and act like it's real gold. Further, the banks create the fool's gold (fake FRB digitized debt) to loan to people who must pay back the loan plus interest with real gold (actual production). FRB, in sum, permits banks to create fool's gold to control the fools.

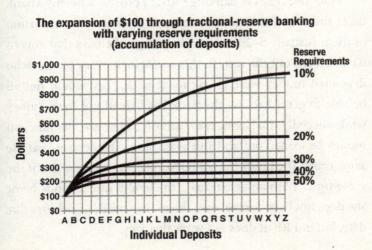

The expansion of $100 through fractional-reserve banking with varying reserve requirements (accumulation of deposits)

The FRB system is the secret to the Financial Matrix, because the ignorance of the masses around creation of debt money is the key to its control and why the latest matrix is the most effective one ever. For instance, the Financial Matrix constantly promotes home ownership because it feeds the growth in the money supply by attaching it to the masses dreams of home ownership. In fact, approximately two-thirds of all US debt money is created through home mortgages acquired by people seeking to "live the American Dream" by "owning" a house. Since 1950, alarmingly, the Financial Matrix has gutted home equity percentages (amount of value remaining after subtracting all mortgage amounts owed), decreasing the equity from over 80% in the early 1950s to just over 30% today. This is nearly a 50% reduction in home equity siphoned out of the USA's $25 trillion housing market. This amounts to around $12.5 trillion (more than the US national debt until a few years ago) of real asset value lost by US citizens and gained by the Financial Matrix. And a similar financial storyline is occurring in all civilized nations.

Fractional reserve banking FRB is a process whereby a bank takes the deposits into the bank and then reserves a portion of them (usually 5–20% depending upon the laws that govern it) and loans out the rest. In this scenario, if every person who deposited money were to ask for it back, they would not all be able to get it because the bank has loaned out their money while allegedly still having it available for their use. But how can money be loaned out and still available to the depositor at the same time? The funds cannot be "owned" by both parties at the same time. With an actual loan, the lender understands he or she does not have control over the money until the debtor's due date, but in FRB, it does not work that way.

Mysteriously, through the fraudulent FRB system, the bank maintains a depositor's access to savings while also loaning the funds out to others. The problem, of course, is the FRB system inflates the money supply (how much so depends upon the reserve ratio chosen) by giving two people (both the depositor and the lender) access to the same money. Indeed, through the use of FRB fiat money (money not backed by gold or silver), the elites have flooded the marketplace with FRB money, causing rapid inflation and rampant injustice. The Financial Matrix was birthed through a web of fractional reserve banking, increasing national debts, and increasing taxes.

Moreover, the crony-capitalistic FRB system sets the interest rates, which have created the boom/bust cycle plaguing modern society. Imagine playing a game of musical chairs where the same chair is fraudulently issued to ten different people without their knowledge. While the music is playing, during the "boom" phase, everyone is happy, and the economy appears to be growing rapidly; however, as debt increases, so too do the prices of everything caused by the predictable inflation. Eventually, the prices of houses, cars, and other big-ticket items outrun the ability of the consumers to service the debt, and the music stops abruptly. The "boom" period has now transformed into the "bust" phase as the highly unstable and inflated money supply bursts because the consumers cannot afford to pay the interest and principal payments on their bloated debt.

Not surprisingly, when the music stops, the consumers discover they do not have actual chairs (real commodity money) to sit down in. Thus, the weakest financially crash to the ground first, but it doesn't stop there. The failure of the banks' marginal loan qualifiers causes a cascading effect (I would say like a row of falling dominoes, but I don't want to mix my metaphors) until only the most conservative financially can survive at all during the bust.

And to add insult to injury, once the FRB system fosters the predictable boom/bust cycle, the boom is credited to the ingenious money controllers, while the bust is blamed on free markets. Apparently, it's a loaded game of heads and tails where heads means the elites win and tails means the masses lose! Although economists the caliber of Ricardo, Mises, and Von Hayek have insisted the FRB system is fraudulent and unstable, it survives through the masses' ignorance and the elites' support. Perhaps British monetary reformer, Michael Rowbotham, described the fraudulent nature of the FRB system the best when he wrote:

> The creation and supply of money is now left almost entirely to banks and other lending institutions. Most people imagine that if they borrow from a bank, they are borrowing other people's money. In fact, when banks and building societies make any loan, they create new money. Money loaned by a bank is not a loan of pre-existent money; money loaned by a bank is additional money created. The stream of money generated by people, businesses and governments constantly borrowing from banks and other lending institutions is relied upon to supply the economy as a whole. Thus the supply of money depends upon people going into debt, and the level of debt within an economy is no more than a measure of the amount of money that has been created.

In effect, today's Financial Matrix relies upon millions of people willingly selling themselves into financial slavery.

For when one combines artificially low centrally controlled interest rates with the FRB system, one has an enticing combination for consumers and entrepreneurs to "borrow money into existence." This money creation, however, leads to inflation, which means, literally, an increase in the money supply. This predictably results in a boom and eventually a bust when inflation raises prices (which always rise as a result of an increased money supply) above a manageable level. At that point, the consumers and entrepreneurs default on the loans they can no longer service, and the bust wipes out value throughout society. These conditions occurred twice during the Greenspan-controlled central banking era (the period of time in which Alan Greenspan was the Chairman of the Federal Reserve Banking System, the institution that sets interest rates, among other things). In both cases, the artificially controlled low interest rates fueled consumers' appetites for speculation and "easy" profits. The Internet bubble increased the NASDAQ nearly by a factor of five during the boom between 1995 and 2000, but it then proceeded to collapse by over 60% from 2000 to 2001.

Unfortunately, those who control the money supply seem to be perpetual optimists who go from failure to failure without learning anything. As a result, when the Twin Towers came crashing down in 2001, Greenspan repeated the same policy that had caused the previous boom/bust cycle. This time, however, money poured into the housing markets, and prices shot up some 50% in just a few short years. Not shockingly, the mortgage companies sought to maximize profits by helping everyone qualify for a home mortgage, even those who didn't have steady jobs. The increase in mortgages exploded the money supply, which further fueled higher priced houses and mortgages. The housing bubble was blowing up. Predictably, however, when the non-qualified borrowers could not make their mortgage payments, the housing bubble and the money supply both collapsed, and the financial house of cards would have followed them had it not been for government bailouts.

My good friends and cofounders of Life George and Jill Guzzardo experienced the 2008 boom/bust cycle firsthand. They purchased prime real estate in Tuscon, Arizona for over one million dollars. They put more than 20% down and intended to pay the rest over five years. However, the bust collapsed the real estate market, and the land wasn't worth half of its former price. The Guzzardos ended up selling the property and still owing over $600,000 for land they no longer owned. Thankfully, the Guzzardos were equipped (by building a huge business asset) to weather the storm and learn valuable FRB lessons. Unfortunately, most others cannot afford these financial lessons. Indeed, for many people, the purchase of their dream home resulted in bankruptcy when the housing market deflated. While practically everyone makes money during the boom, most end up losing everything in the bust. Unbelievably, however, when the negative effects of the boom/bust cycle hit, the main group the government protects is the FRB system that created the issue in the first place. In other words, the fractional reserve banks reap profit during the boom and secure protection during the bust.

Fractional reserve banking, in sum, is a key aspect for profits and control in the Financial Matrix because it is government-sponsored activity that allows bankers to make low-interest loans to the government and the people without actually having the money to do so. Loans are created out of thin air as mere digits on a computer screen. However, the productive entrepreneurs and workers must pay back these loans with real production dollars. The Financial Matrix is so ubiquitous because it provides fake loans to be paid back with interest from real money earned from real production. In my opinion, the best long-term strategy against FRB and the Financial Matrix is for Americans to educate themselves on a concept called Privatized Banking. This thought process gives individuals, and business owners an alternative financial institution to utilize for their cash flow and a better temporary headquarters to store their safe liquid cash until needed. In this supercharged savings account, you still retain liquidity, use and total control of your money, and a dramatically higher rate of return, along with numerous other benefits not found at commercial banks. Most importantly, this financial institution *cannot* inflate the money supply from your deposits and enslave future generations by creating money out of thin air. When enough households engage in the process of Privatized Banking, the power of banks to multiply the money supply will be dramatically reduced and the Financial Matrix will eventually collapse.

APPENDIX 2

WHAT ARE THE THREE HISTORICAL MATRICES OF CONTROL?

The Three Financial Matrices

As stated earlier in the book, the Financial Matrix was not the aristocracy's first matrix of control but rather the third one (based on the third factor of production) created after the first two matrices (based on the first two factors of production) collapsed. Most people are familiar with the other two matrices of control, the Physical Matrix (labor slavery) and the Feudal Matrix (land serfdom). The Greeks and Romans wrote about liberty and justice extensively; they also hypocritically exercised the Physical Matrix to enslave defeated foes. The slaves were forced to work while the conquerors, who disdained physical work, enjoyed the liberty to speak, write, and lead. The Physical Matrix was a system of control in which the aristocracy (the strong) forced the masses (the weak) to toil away in slavery and obscurity. The Physical Matrix was the preferred method of control throughout antiquity until something changed in the late Roman Empire. That change was the influence of Christianity on the social norms of Roman society. Whereas slavery was previously acceptable, Christian doctrine taught that all were created equal before an almighty God. Since all fellow believers were brothers and sisters in Christ, it became increasingly difficult to rationalize how a Christian could enslave a fellow brother or sister. (Unfortunately, the later discovery of America restored

European rationalizations, which led to the Physical Matrix enslavement of people from Africa.) Thus, without the moral support in European society, the Physical Matrix collapsed under its own weight during the Middle Ages.

Not surprisingly, however, the aristocrats sought an alternative matrix of control to replace it. Since labor could no longer be controlled directly, perhaps the aristocracy could instead do indirectly what it could no longer do directly. Predictably, almost as if the aristocracy understood the three factors of production and crossed off the first one (labor) only to move on to the next one (land), the aristocracy built the Feudal Matrix by owning and controlling all the land during Europe's Middle Ages. The Feudal Matrix (land serfdom) was a system of control that empowered the aristocrats (kings, princes, and lords) with land, while the serfs were forced to serve a lord in order to survive.

Feudalism (the Feudal Matrix) was, in essence, a system that allowed the aristocrats to promise the serfs protection in exchange for the serfs working the aristocrats' lands. The new matrix provided serfs the land they needed to live for a land tax amounting to around 50% of their agricultural production. Furthermore, the serfs agreed to work their lord's fields several days a week, since the aristocrats rarely, if ever, worked their own fields. The serfs, having nowhere else to go and not having the strength to resist such tyranny, simply submitted to the Feudal Matrix. Although the serfs were technically no longer slaves, they weren't exactly free either; high taxes and forced immobility permitted the aristocrats to indirectly control the serfs' labor by directly controlling all the land. Generations of serfs would live and die on the same piece of land performing basically the same work as their forefathers. Feudalism in Europe ended the Physical Matrix slavery (control of the first factor of production, labor) only to birth the Feudal Matrix serfdom (control of the second factor of production, land).

Finally, however, during the late Middle Ages, the reintroduction of gold and silver destroyed the economics of feudalism, as the serfs no longer needed to live on the lords' land. The serfs migrated to the growing cities, where they became butchers, bakers, and candlestick makers. In the city air, serfs could breathe free. The peasants, instead of being stuck to the land, sold their services for gold and silver (commodity money) and then traded the commodity money to purchase other items necessary for survival. Commodity money and free cities allowed the serfs to live without the lords' land, and predictably, the Feudal Matrix collapsed. The serfs could no longer be controlled by the aristocrats, and now the Physical and Feudal Matrices were, for all practical purposes, extinct.

However, there was still one remaining factor of production (capital) the aristocrats could seek to control in order to build another matrix. The battle between society's gold standard commodity money and the aristocrats' fiat standard debt money began in earnest. Simply put, money was created by society's members as a measurement of exchange of values. The following several paragraphs are an attempt to simplify a complicated subject. Thankfully, it's not crucial to understand all of this when reading it for the first time, but I want to include it so that people have access to the truth of our current financial system.

APPENDIX 3
WHAT IS MONEY?

The Creation of Money

Money was created by society as the most marketable commodity to use as society's medium of exchange. This improved the speed at which goods and services were traded in a win-win fashion within society. This benefited all producers of goods. Precious metals, in particular gold and silver, were the preferred forms of money because they were scarce, easily divisible, mobile, and universally recognized. And since precious metals have a fixed quantity (they cannot be created out of thin air) and are difficult to mine, inflation (any increase in the total money supply) was low and predictable. Indeed, the rebirth of the gold standard commodity money fueled the growth of capitalism by increasing the division of labor and trade between peoples. Remarkably, for nearly four hundred years, commodity money led to the creation of more wealth for more people than at any time in recorded history.

Of course, the aristocrats attempted various methods to manipulate the money supply (debasement and fractional reserve banking), but the gold standard tied their hands. Indeed, any time the people suspected the aristocrats of foul play, they could demand all payments in gold, forcing the aristocrats to pay in commodity money rather than in the fraudulently increased paper debt money. The gold standard acted as an automatic regulator to protect the masses against the manipulations of the elites because it forced the elites to redeem their paper debt money in gold commodity money whenever the paper holder demanded it. This on-demand gold standard redemption policy tempered the aristocrats' inflation manipulation ability because the elites feared the masses would cause a run on their banks if they suspected fraudulent overprinting of paper notes compared to actual gold reserves. The gold standard was the last line of defense to protect the people from the elites' matrix of control over the third factor of production (capital).

Unfortunately, with the start of World War I, the elites finally smashed through the gold standard and achieved their four-hundred-year objective: the birth of the Financial Matrix through control of the third factor of production (capital). The liberty that had expanded for four hundred years now began its long contraction in the vise grip of fiat debt money (money not backed by precious metals) and fractional reserve banking.

True, the wealth created over those four hundred years was not lost overnight, but slowly, painfully, and inexorably, debt money replaced commodity money, and control replaced liberty. Economist Ludwig von Mises noted, "Just as the sound money policy of gold standard advocates went hand in hand with liberalism, free trade, capitalism and peace, so is inflationism part and parcel of imperialism, militarism, protectionism, statism and socialism." For example, in the chart below, notice how, under the gold standard, the money supply inflated with fractional reserve banking, but also contracted when the people refused paper and demanded gold. However, once central banks' paper replaced gold, deflation was a thing of the past, and the money supply has skyrocketed as displayed below. The gold standard, in sum, checked the worst behaviors of the bank and protected the people. This, in essence, is why the big banks lobbied for a central bank and the end of the gold standard, for the gold-standard inhibited their ability to inflate the money supply and defraud the people.

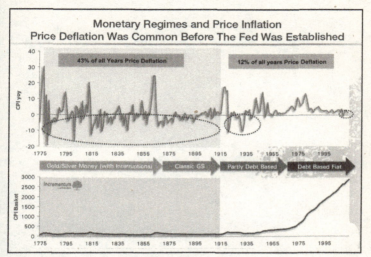

Source: Incrementum AG, Liechtenstein

The aristocrats' Financial Matrix created a system of indirect control of the masses' labor through the direct control of the medium of exchange (money) needed by all using the capitalistic system. One can easily see the damage caused by the Financial Matrix by studying the lost value of the US dollar since the 1913 creation of the Federal Reserve banking system in the United States. The value of one US dollar in 1913 is less than four cents today as displayed in the previous graph.

FINANCIAL FITNESS PROGRAM

*You've Worked Enough for Money,
Now It's Time to Get It Working for You!*

FREE PERSONAL WEBSITE

SIGN UP AND TAKE ADVANTAGE OF THESE FREE FEATURES:

- Personal website
- Take your custom assessment test
- Build your own profile
- Share milestones and successes with partners and friends
- Post videos and photos
- Receive daily info "nuggets"

FINANCIAL FITNESS BASIC PROGRAM

The first program to teach all three aspects of personal finance: defense, offense, and playing field. Learn the simple, easy-to-apply principles that can help you shore up your resources, get out of debt, and build stability for a more secure future. It's all here, including a comprehensive book, companion workbook, and 8 audios that amplify the teachings from the books.

Also available DIGITALLY!

financialfitnessinfo.com

FINANCIAL FITNESS MASTER CLASS

Buy it once and use it forever! Designed to provide a continual follow-up to the principles learned in the Basic Program, this ongoing educational support offers over 6 hours of video and over 14 hours of audio instruction that walk you through the workbook, step by step. Perfect for individual or group study.
6 videos, 15 audios

FINANCIAL FITNESS SERVICES

The Financial Fitness Services subscription provides tools to help implement the theory taught in the Financial Fitness training materials. This value-packed monthly subscription provides the following services:

- Mobile expense tracker and budgeting for continued organization
- Aggregated coupons for saving money
- Prepaid legal coverage for getting and keeping your affairs in order
- Identity monitoring and theft protection to keep you safe
- Credit Monitoring to keep you in good standing

Get your finances on track toward security and prosperity with these amazing, market-proven services all in one handy and affordable monthly subscription!

FINANCIAL FITNESS BULLION RESERVE

In the words of author Fred Schwed, "The science of economics has reached a point where further confusion is impossible." Nowhere is this more evident, perhaps, than in the consideration of whether or not individuals should own gold as part of their investment portfolio. If you've made the decision to add physical gold bullion to your own holdings, we invite you to consider the Financial Fitness Bullion Reserve as your trusted source for certified, convenient, competitively priced (meaning low commissioned), and elegantly packaged physical gold.

Available for a one-time purchase, or as part of an ongoing accumulation program, or both, Financial Fitness Bullion Reserve products allow you to search no further for trustworthy, real, physical gold.

financialfitnessinfo.com

THE WEALTH HABITS SERIES

The Wealth Habits series is designed to help you prosper through consistent, ongoing, simple, and enjoyable financial literacy education. You will learn timeless principles about how to better handle your money, and timely commentary on the current economic forces affecting the "playing field" upon which we all must participate. Small doses of information  applied consistently over time can produce enormous results through the formation of new and profitable habits. This is what the Wealth Habits series is all about.

The Wealth Habits series will put you in a unique position. You will know something that only a few people in the world know. You will know the principles of financial fitness. You have the power to not only develop financial fitness but also to positively impact the lives of those around you. And the time to act is NOW.

LEARN TO NOT ONLY *SURVIVE*, BUT *THRIVE* DURING TOUGH ECONOMIC TIMES!

BEYOND FINANCIAL FITNESS PROGRAM

The original Financial Fitness Program taught all three aspects of personal finance:defense, offense, and playing field. Now, the long anticipated Beyond Financial Fitness builds on that platform by teaching how to maximize the potential of your various streams of income by properly accumulating an ever-growing portfolio of cash-flow-producing assets.

Drawn from many of the greatest minds in the history of personal finance, the Beyond Financial Fitness Program teaches you to gain mastery over your money once and for all and includes a comprehensive book, audio version of the book, a companion workbook, 4 audios, and 2 DVDs. Bookmark and decal also included.

You've worked enough for money, now it's time to get it working for you!

Also available DIGITALLY!

TOTAL PERSONAL DEVELOPMENT SUBSCRIPTION

Your All-In-One Personal Development Product

Based on the *New York Times* bestselling book *Launching a Leadership Revolution*, the LLR Corporate education program is designed not to train employees but to develop leaders. Leadership development is arguably the single most important investment any company can make. The leader creates the culture; the culture delivers the results.

Life Library

The Life Library is your round-the-clock video resource for all the best talks created by Life's content contributors – you never have to be quiet in this library!

The Leadership Platform

The Leadership Platform contains a massive array of audio and video content, as well as articles and book summaries, from the top business and thought leaders in the world today.

Audio Books

Reading just got easier! Life is pleased to include our top-selling Obstaclés Press audio books to all Total Personal Development subscribers. They will receive unlimited access to our top-selling audio books either on their desktops, laptops, or mobile devices. Easy, portable, and under your control, now you don't have to spend extra money to get the audio books you want.

Language Learning

Let Total Personal Development be your language lab. Select from more than 90 language options and learn with specialized software that's outcome driven and personalized, with measurable results. Learn your new language faster and better with training that uses proven methods and breakthrough technology.

Rascal Radio

Rascal Radio is the world's first online/mobile customizable personal development radio station. A lot like Pandora does with music, Rascal Radio randomizes talks by some of the world's top leadership experts, life coaches, bestselling authors, and speakers. Sort by speaker, category, and language to create customized stations that speak just to you!

Sales Training

Whether you consider yourself a great salesperson or want to become one, professional sales training from Life is convenient, timely and affordable. Learn about all the many aspects of professional sales, including basic and advance selling techniques, customer service, contacting, and more.

mainhomepage.com

CORPORATE DEVELOPMENT PROGRAM

The 6-month Leadership Development Program Designed to Transform the Corporate World!

Based on the *New York Times* bestseller *Launching a Leadership Revolution*, the LLR Corporate Education Program is designed not just to train our customers' employees but to **gradually** and **effectively** help them develop **their existing talent into engaged, contributing, go-to leaders** and systemically **create a permanent culture of leadership** in their organizations.

With several programs involving interactive learning, progress tracking, audio, visual, and group learning, as well as facilitator's materials and guides, the LLR Corporate Education Program has been **successfully utilized** in some of the largest companies in the world, as well as professional sports teams, schools, and even as coursework in colleges and universities.

LLRC Subscription Programs

LLR Corporate Education Program Course 1 (6 Sessions)
This is where Life's corporate revolution began. Firmly establish a leadership culture throughout your entire workforce with the 6 monthly sessions of LLRC Course 1.

LLR Corporate Education Program Course 2 (6 Sessions)
Keep up the leadership momentum LLRC Course 1 started, and build on it with LLRC Course 2 to further increase employee engagement, productivity, and retention.

LLR Corporate Education Program Course 3 (6 Sessions)
LLRC Course 3 shifts gears a little bit and begins applying the concepts learned in Courses 1 and 2 by considering an interesting and very broad array of case studies.

LLR Corporate Education 12-Month Program Courses 1 and 2 (12 Sessions)
Establish and solidify a leadership culture throughout your workforce over the period of a year with the LLRC 12-Month Education Program, which includes all of the materials from LLRC Courses 1 and 2. Definitely a longer term option for the savvy employer.

LLR Corporate Education 18-Month Program Courses 1, 2, and 3 (18 Sessions)
The momentum will stay in full effect with the LLRC 18-Month Education Program, which includes all of the materials for LLRC Courses 1, 2, and 3. Experience lasting results and effectiveness that allow for ongoing success and help to attract high-caliber new talent to your organization.